The Churches and

of the Parish of Tidenham

Their History and Architecture

Edited by Carol Clammer and Keith Underwood

tidenham historical group

This book is dedicated to the memory of those members of the Tidenham Historical Group who contributed to the early research but are sadly no longer with us:
Rene Cook, Anthony James, Mervyn Prothero, Joyce Pullinger, Mercedes and Linda Waters, Rose Evans and Eric Wiles.

tidenham historical group

Published by Tidenham Historical Group
2 Westbourne Villas, Sedbury Lane, Tutshill, Chepstow NP16 7DZ
E-mail: info@tidenhamhistory.co.uk

ISBN 978 0 9928722 0 5

Typeset in Garamond and Helvetica
Designed by Alan Kittridge
Printed by Tower Print Ltd, Caerphilly

AWARDS
FOR ALL

CONTENTS

BROCKWEIR

RIVER WYE

A466

B4428

22

23

TIDENHAM CHASE

24

STROAT

B4428 **21**

20 TIDENHAM

LANCAUT **19**

WOODCROFT **18**

16
17

A48

15

TUTSHILL

14

SEDBURY

12 **13**

A466

CHEPSTOW

11

A48

RIVER SEVERN

BEACHLEY

7 **10**
9 **8** **3** **6**
4
5 **2**

1

M48

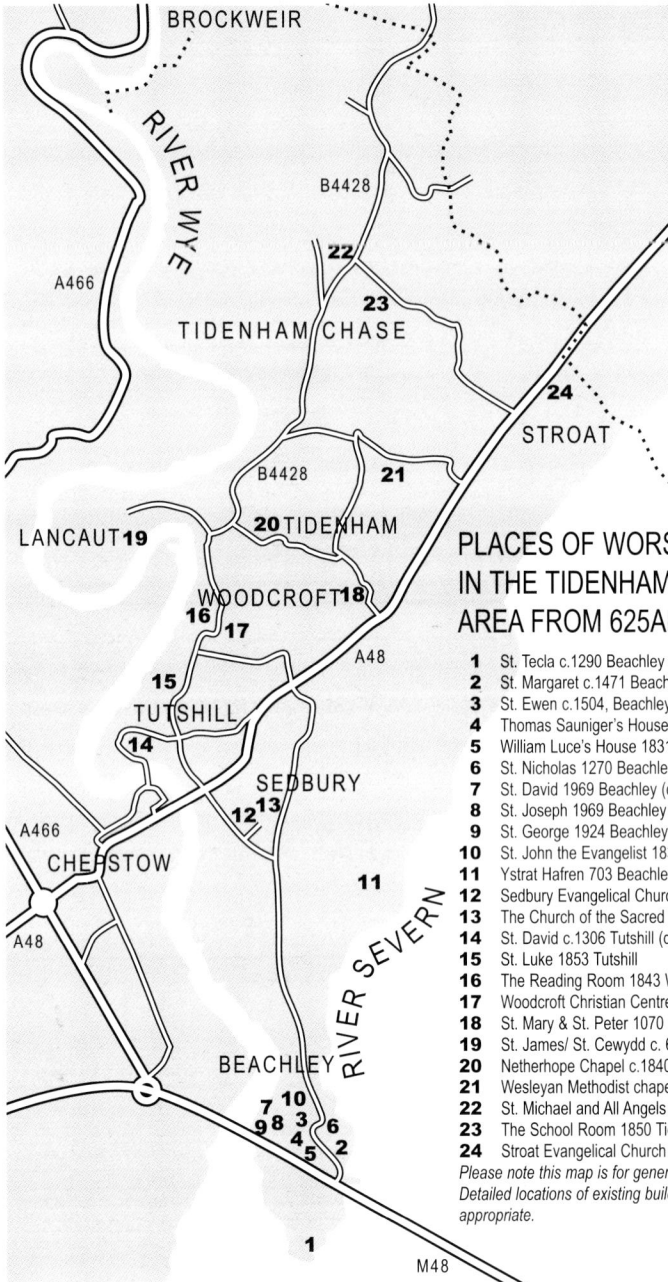

PLACES OF WORSHIP IN THE TIDENHAM PARISH AREA FROM 625AD

1   St. Tecla c.1290 Beachley (ruin)
2   St. Margaret c.1471 Beachley (disappeared)
3   St. Ewen c.1504, Beachley (disappeared)
4   Thomas Sauniger's House 1820 Beachley (disappeared)
5   William Luce's House 1831 Beachley (disappeared)
6   St. Nicholas 1270 Beachley (disappeared)
7   St. David 1969 Beachley (converted)
8   St. Joseph 1969 Beachley (disappeared)
9   St. George 1924 Beachley
10 St. John the Evangelist 1833 Beachley (converted)
11 Ystrat Hafren 703 Beachley (disappeared)
12 Sedbury Evangelical Church 1951
13 The Church of the Sacred Heart 1939 Sedbury
14 St. David c.1306 Tutshill (disappeared)
15 St. Luke 1853 Tutshill
16 The Reading Room 1843 Woodcroft (disappeared)
17 Woodcroft Christian Centre 1887
18 St. Mary & St. Peter 1070 Tidenham
19 St. James/ St. Cewydd c. 625 Lancaut (ruin)
20 Netherhope Chapel c.1840 (converted)
21 Wesleyan Methodist chapel 1836 Boughspring (converted)
22 St. Michael and All Angels 1888 Tidenham Chase
23 The School Room 1850 Tidenham Chase
24 Stroat Evangelical Church 1889
Please note this map is for general guidance only and not to scale.
Detailed locations of existing buildings are given in the text where
appropriate.

FOREWORD

The Tidenham Historical Group was founded on January 31st 1990 and has been involved since that date in a variety of projects connected with the whole range of parish history. The group membership had changed over the years but the research has continued and this book encapsulates just one part of that work which we hope will make a lasting contribution to the history of the Parish of Tidenham, and the area surrounding it. We are indebted to the National Lottery Awards for All Programme for the initial funding.

In one modest volume this book gives a unique overview of the history, significance and architecture of the various places of worship past and present in the parish, as well as some of the fascinating people who were involved in those buildings' social history and development. Some twenty-five places of worship, large and small, formal and less formal have existed over the period of this parish's history from AD625 until the last building was constructed in 1988. The history of some is limited to a one-line reference in ancient documents, while others benefit from a wide range of detailed historical documents. As it was local people who used the buildings and brought them alive, the book reflects human aspects of their history throughout: wealthy benefactors who supported the poor in the area; individuals who died whilst working on a church or for their country; those who put their name to a petition; even a whole congregational community given eleven days to move out of their homes. All played their part in this particular history just as the present inhabitants continue to do.

The places of worship are presented in date order of their building or origins. We have used modern place names for consistency whilst acknowledging that some names have changed many times throughout the period of this history.

After an introduction, most chapters describe the history of the place of worship, go on to describe any appropriate architectural features and many end with a guided a tour of the building, including an Ordnance Survey grid reference where appropriate. We hope that the readers will find the information in this book as absorbing as we did whilst producing it and will be encouraged to appreciate the sites described in a new and different light.

KEITH UNDERWOOD, GROUP CO-ORDINATOR

1

EARLY HISTORY AND LOST PLACES OF WORSHIP

The parish of Tidenham with Beachley and Lancaut forms a triangle, with the River Severn on one side and the River Wye on a second. The third side is bounded by the parishes of Hewelsfield and Woolaston. The parish has a total land area of 29 square kilometres and is approximately twelve kilometres from North to South and five kilometres at its widest point, with high cliffs forming much of the Western boundary along the River Wye. The highest ground, at 237 metres, is across the Tidenham Chase and the remainder slopes down eastwards towards lower ground by the River Severn.

Until the end of the Bronze Age at around 900BC the sea did not come much further than Cardiff. Peat formed at each side of the River Severn which wound its way to the sea. This marshy peat grew to a possible thickness of twelve feet but with the rise in sea level that followed, the peat was compressed, possibly to little over a metre in thickness. From then on there was gradual erosion of the coast line. The parish has been occupied by prehistoric people as evidenced by the discovery of a Stone Age axe found at Boughspring, a Bronze Age barrow on Tidenham Chase and a burial cist in Beachley. There were Iron Age Hill forts at Spital Meend, on Netherhope Lane and Coomesbury Wood (which is now the National Diving Centre).

The Romans built a major road from Gloucester to Caerwent passing through the parish, largely following the line of the current A48, then crossing the river Wye well to the north of the current bridge. Roman pottery was found during road improvements at Stroat, an altar stone, believed to be Roman, was found on the Chase and coins were found in two other places. They built a secondary road leading down to Beachley and the crossing point to Aust and there is evidence of a Roman Villa at Boughspring and a Roman site in Sedbury Park, possibly with kilns.

Opposite:
Detail of a fine
1894 window in St
Luke's church
showing Christ
with young
children.
Liz Pitman

The evidence for occupation in the Dark Ages of the fifth to seventh centuries AD is scarce, but burials of the period were inserted into the ruined Roman Villa. There was a manor of Tidenham existing in Welsh hands after the battle of Dyrham in AD 577 and the Book of Llandaff records that the Abbot of Lan Ceuid witnessed a grant of land by Athrwys, King of Gwent, in 625 AD. Tidenham was in Saxon ownership by the time Offa built his Dyke to keep out the Welsh circa AD 784 but, significantly, the land at Lancaut and Beachley was outside the Dyke, being occupied by Welsh fishermen.

It is at Lancaut that there is the first evidence, circa 625 AD, for a Christian church in this area, dedicated to the Celtic **St. Cewydd** to serve a Welsh fishing population in an area that was later to become part of the parish of Tidenham. Shortly afterwards another church of **Ystrat Hafren** was built at Beachley, near the minor Roman road and by the river Severn. It was granted by Morgan ap Arthrys, King of Glywyssing in south-east Wales, to Berthguin, Bishop of Llandaff in 703 AD, (as was St. Cewydd's at Lancaut). Unfortunately nothing is known of this church's location.

Then in 878 AD Hywel ap Rhys, king of Glywyssing, re-granted both Beachley and Lancaut churches to Llandaff. There they stayed well into the middle of the tenth century. A tenth century charter refers to small areas of land adjacent to the River Wye left by treaty for the use of Welsh fishermen and river navigators and it was probably this that resulted in Lancaut remaining a separate "Welsh" parish for a while longer.

In Saxon and medieval times the settlements other than Lancaut appeared to be concentrated in the east and south of Tidenham parish and are represented by the farmsteads lying scattered along the Gloucester-Chepstow road and the road leading southwards from it towards Beachley. Just as Lancaut had its small settlement concentrated on fishing the river Wye, the river passage at Beachley provided the reason for the only other nucleated hamlet in the parish at this time.

There was a manor-house on Tidenham manor recorded before the Norman Conquest of 1066. It was not unusual in those days for land to be moved from one wealthy landowner to another and during the middle of the tenth century both Lancaut and Beachley were transferred to the Diocese of Hereford when King Edwys granted the large manor of Tidenham, Stroat, Bishton, Sedbury, Beachley, and Lancaut to Wulfgar the Abbot of Bath in 956 AD who, in turn, then leased the territory for life to Archbishop Stigand in about 1061-65.

He then forfeited it in 1070 after the Norman Conquest when William FitzOsbern the Earl of Hereford, on behalf of William the Conqueror, established the Marcher lordship of Striguil (that later became known as Chepstow) with its powerbase in the castle. The large parcel of land then passed to the Earl and it was in this period that the imposing parish church of St Mary and St Peter at Tidenham was built high on a hill overlooking the river in about 1070. The history of this church is described in Chapter 5.

The territory was in the King's hands by the time of the Doomsday records of 1086 with the exception of two sections, a small part of Tidenham with Woolaston held by William de Eu, and a part of Tidenham with Madgetts, held by Roger de Laci. Both these areas were forfeited around 1093 and returned to the King. Lancaut remained a separate, relatively isolated, Welsh parish with one church re-named St James, and rebuilt to conform to the catholic influence of the Norman lord FitzOsbern, as described in Chapter 3.

Beachley on the other hand, as a vital crossing point across the river Severn to Aust under the influence first of a Saxon and catholic royal manor and then Striguil, apparently had several churches. It also had its own manor. There is a reference in 1270 is to a "recluse" at the chapel of **St Nicholas** at Beachley, who received corn and alms from Tidenham Manor. A further reference in 1273 says that the same alms were received by Patrick, chaplain of St. Nicholas. This may be referring to the chapel or church established before 703, or to one of the other chapels or chantries in Beachley known to have been in existence in the Middle Ages. Although there is no written record of the hermit's cell on what is now known as St Tecla's island off the tip of Beachley peninsula until 1290, it is believed that the cell may well have been built many years before. Chapter 2 describes the history of this hermit's cell in more detail.

One of the most intriguing mysteries is the exact whereabouts of the early **St David's Chapel**. The dedication to St David is an interesting one, since Welsh saints were not particularly popular with the Anglo-Norman hierarchy. In 1855 Wakeman described the location of the wooden mediaeval bridge over the river Wye at Chepstow and *"next to it on the Gloucestershire side, stood the little chapel of St David. Part of the walls, with the lower portion of the east window and the entrance door were standing within my remembrance. All traces of it have now disappeared and even the site is known but to a few of the present generation."* The mediaeval bridge is believed to have been in roughly the same location as the current cast iron bridge and led directly from the town of Chepstow, across the river Wye, to link up with the route of the steep old road, known as the Old Hill.

There are also references in 1841 by the Society of Antiquarians to a *"Chapel House Farm, at the Gloucestershire end of Chepstow*

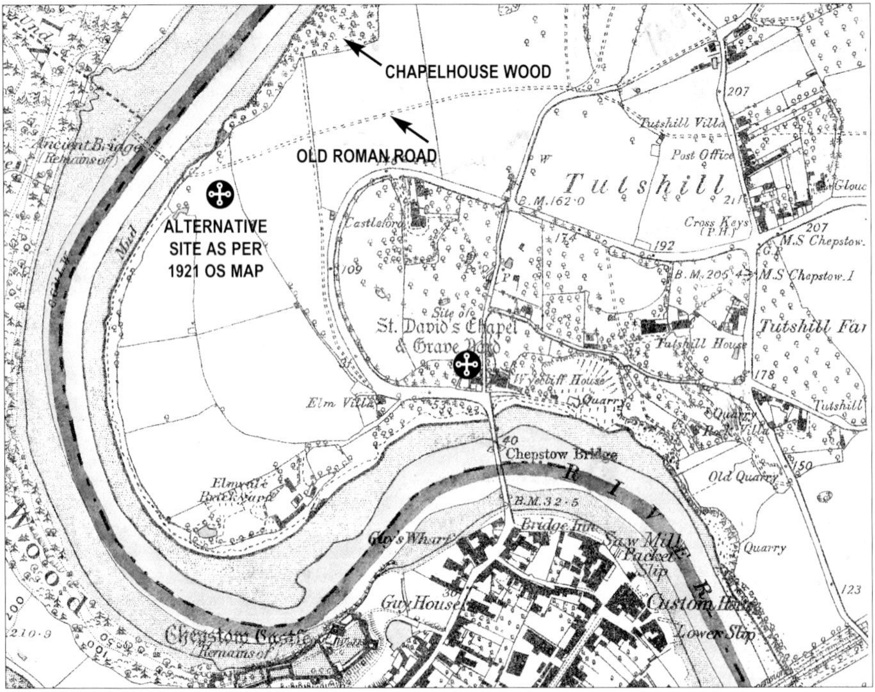

Labels on map:
CHAPELHOUSE WOOD
OLD ROMAN ROAD
ALTERNATIVE SITE AS PER 1921 OS MAP

Fig. 1 Detail from a map of Tidenham parish dated 1880 showing the two possible locations of the chapel of St David's - juxta - pontem. *Tidenham History Group*

Bridge...[which] commemorates the former chapel... some remains of which existed about 1814". According to a map of the parish dated around 1880, the chapel was situated to the west of the Old Hill leading directly up from Chepstow Bridge to Tutshill. This seems in accordance with the *Inquisitio Post Mortem* following the death of Roger Bigod, Earl of Norfolk, which cites a Chantry Chapel of St. David *juxta pontem*, (near or next to the bridge), where priests were paid to sing, or chant, the Mass prayers on behalf of travellers or the wealthy. A later second edition Ordinance Survey map of 1902 also shows the chapel below Castleford House and to the west of the old road leading down from Tutshill to Chepstow Bridge. All of these sources seem to agree that the location of the chapel was probably somewhere to the rear of the gardens of the cottages facing Chepstow bridge adjacent to the Old Hill. However, some other sources locate the chapel near the course of the old Roman road near the river bank close to the site of the ancient bridge, a claim further complicated by the name of the nearby Chapel House Wood. (see Fig. 1)

Wherever it was located, it possibly did not start life as a chantry chapel house but may originally have served as a house for the sick "next to Striguil" which was said to have assarted, (converted to arable), twelve acres of forest land in Tidenham Manor before 1282. By 1306, the year of the Earl of Norfolk's death, the warden of the Hospital of St David "near Chepstow bridge" was holding 28 acres of waste land in the manor and was paying "as in terms £4s 8d yearly". He also held a half acre of land for which he paid 2d. The property later actually passed to Striguil Priory, which until the reign of Edward IV, was an "alien" priory whose dues were paid to the owning body, the Benedictine Abbey of Cormeilles in France.

A chapel on a main thoroughfare could easily have then developed into a chantry where a traveller could pay to have mass said or sung for his soul, perhaps to insure against the rigours of the journey. In an age of plague, sick people would also pay for the safe passage of their souls. There would have been be a resident priest, possibly more than one, and the Benedictine monks of Striguil might also have served the Chapel.

The Wye bridge linking Chepstow and Tutshill with the entrance to the Old Hill between the cottages on the left and the house on the right. The location of the old chapel of St David could be in the wooded area above the cottages.
R. Clammer

Other chapels in Beachley are thought to have been built for the same purpose for travellers using the passage to Aust. In 1398 a burgess from Bristol left money for a priest to celebrate mass for him in the chapel of Beachley. Another testator left money in 1471 for obits, (prayers for the dead), and also a silver bowl for use as a chalice in the chapel of **St Margaret**, at Beachley. This chapel may have been a private oratory, for which inhabitants of Beachley were given a licence, possibly in 1446, but sadly there is little evidence of the location of this place of worship and further research is required.

In his will of 1504 John Hopkins left land and rent non-specifically to '*the church of Beachley*'. A chapel which stood next to the Passage House in 1573 dedicated to **St. Ewen**, was demolished by 1779. By 1624 Beachley was a fairly compact settlement with a population of probably less than a hundred which did not increase until the nineteenth century. Thus as the 18th century gave way to the 19th, the parish church of St Peter and St Mary at Tidenham and the chapel of St James at Lancaut served the entire population of the Tidenham parish.

It was at this point that the development of a variety of worshipping groups occurred in the area. On June 5th 1820, Benjamin Taylor, a Methodist preacher from Chepstow, used the **house of Thomas Sauniger** as a protestant place of worship in Beachley. Later, William Williams of Chepstow lodged a request to the Bishop's Court and received assent on June 18th 1831 from the Bishop of Gloucester for a Beachley **house occupied by a William Luce** to be used as a place of worship by Protestant Dissenters. Although a tithe map of 1843 shows a piece of land described as a *garden* in Beachley owned by one Thomas Saniger, nothing remains of the whereabouts or the longevity of these buildings. Such was the impact of these requests on the vicar of Tidenham, the Reverend Thomas Thomas, that he instigated rapid negotiations with the wealthy and influential in Beachley to counter the effects of competition, as described in Chapter 7.

The Hockaday Abstracts of 1844 identify a **Reading Room** built at Woodcroft in 1843 as being used for worship by Baptists and others under a Chepstow minister in 1851, when it claimed a congregation of between seventy and ninety. It was presumably the Independent Reading Room recorded in the parish until 1870 by Kelly's Directory. The location of this room remains a mystery but a later chapter describes the impact and the aftermath of this lost place of worship on the village of Woodcroft and its inhabitants.

As further research is done, yet more lost buildings may well emerge. However, the ensuing chapters describe, in chronological order of the building date, the churches and chapels and other buildings of worship which can still be seen or which have a visual record.

Ordnance Survey Grid reference: Sheet 162 scale 1:50 000
Please note that since the buildings have disappeared and their locations open to discussion, the following grid-references are approximate. Both are on private land.
ST MARGARET'S/ ST EWENS 553907
ST DAVID 549911

View of the chapel of St Tecla from the old Severn Bridge at high tide showing its remote location. *R Clammer*

2 THE CHAPEL OF ST TECLA, BEACHLEY

HISTORY

The scant ruins of one of the earliest churches in the parish perch on the rock crest of the seaweed covered St Tecla's Island off the southern tip of the Beachley peninsula. Although there is no written record of the hermit's cell on the island until 1290 when a Benedictine monk was licensed to celebrate in the chapel of St. Tryak of Beachley, it is thought that the cell was in existence much earlier. The name changed many times, including Twrog, Traigyl, Tryacle, Teriacus, Treacle, Tiriocus, Turocus, Tyrioc, Thryiac, Trioc, Tiriac, Tryak, and Tryor.

It is a further hundred years to the next reference in 1394, when an exchange is recorded between Margaret Countess of Norfolk who presented, or appointed, John Pomfreyt as warden of the chapel of St Tryor, and John Prophete in the Chichester Diocese. Later, in 1402 John Prophete became Dean of Hereford and there is a record of John Chaudeler being appointed to the chapel of St. Tirioc in the Diocese of Hereford. The appointment was in the King's gift and Prophete had custody of the land of the late Duke of Norfolk who was tenant-in-chief to Richard II. In 1404 John Bremor was appointed by Thomas Earl Marshall to the free chapel of the parish church of St. Thyriac, vacant on the resignation of John Chaudeler. With yet another version of the name, 1407 saw John Prentys appointed to the free chapel of Trioc in the Diocese of Hereford.

The next reference is in 1421 when priest Richard Sandrey was instituted by the Archbishop of Canterbury to the chapel of St. Tiriac in Forest Deanery. Forty three years later in 1464, William Herbert, a native of Usk, was presented by John ap Thomelyn, the local patron and Lord of Beachley, to the chapel of St. Tirioc again in the Hereford diocese. In 1489, Hugh David was instituted following Herbert's death, by the Bishop of Hereford and presented by Thomelyn. The last recorded presentation was by the Earl of Worcester, Lord of Tidenham, in 1519. In 1535 the chapel was reported as being useless because it stood in the sea and no further use was made of it.

As the river channels and sea levels changed over the centuries, the chapel became more isolated and inaccessible. It was already a ruin in

Chapel Rock at the Mouth of the Wye
CAPELLA SANCTI TERIACI ANACHORITÆ.

the eighteenth century when in 1750 a proposal by Ralph Allen of Prior Park, Bath, to rebuild the chapel was thwarted by the Lewis family from St Pierre who owned the site. The next recorded visitor was Eleanor Ormerod, one of the daughters of George Ormerod, the owner of Sedbury Park and a local antiquarian. She and her brothers clambered over the slippery rocks on more than one occasion during the 1840s, to picnic and to record the details of what remained of the chapel. Her brother, Henry Mere Ormerod, apparently made a drawing of its plan and she records in her autobiography the measurements of 31'6" length by 14'16" width, with the walls approximately 3ft thick. It would be impossible today to come to that conclusion, so destroyed and eroded is the site. Her own sketch, however, seems to show the ruin much as we see it today, with a better preserved doorhead and two massive pieces of fallen masonry.

In her autobiography Miss Omerod speaks of *"the few but massive remains of the Hermitage and Chapels"* and *"this little but massive knot of buildings"* surviving in 1873. In the absence of a much-needed archaeological survey, any hypothetical restoration can only be conjectural, but the orientation seems certain and tallies with the Ormerod measurements.

There was originally no doubt some sort of causeway for access but the ferocity and strength of the tides and severe storms explain the considerable erosion that has taken place, even since Miss Omerod's day.

THE BUILDING

The orientation of the building is virtually identical with that of the church of St James (or the chapel of St. Ceuidd) at Lancaut, reflecting their similarity in age. The numbers in brackets refer to the plan of the chapel in Figure 2.

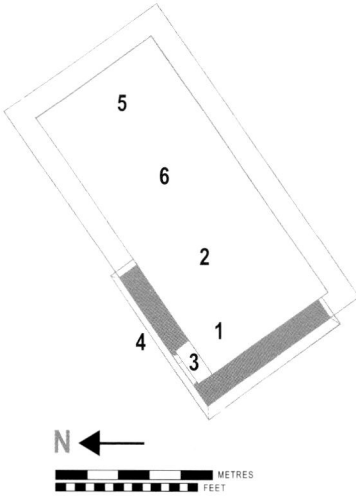

Fig. 2 Chapel of St Tecla, Beachley

On a visit to the island in 2000, in the company of the local lifeboat service, a member of the Tidenham Historical Group observed: *"Once on the island you climb up the beach to the remains of the Chapel almost overshadowed by the modern navigation light* **(1)** *located in what was probably the chancel area* **(2)***. Its Romanesque door* **(3)** *has lost most of the voussoirs, (wedge shaped blocks), that made up the arch, but a search along the beach was rewarding, since lost stones lay there.*

One remaining doorway arch survives and the original jambs with rebates against which the door closed. The remaining walls **(4)** *are battered at the base, that towards the west quite considerably. The conjectural outline of the building based on the Ormerod measurements, seems to show that the Sanctuary* **(6)** *and the Altar* **(5)** *would have been sited where the beach now is."*

A stone from one of the collapsed doorway supports of the chapel of St Tecla, showing the carved door jamb on the left.
K Underwood

The surviving walls and door arch of the chapel of St Tecla in 2001.
K Underwood

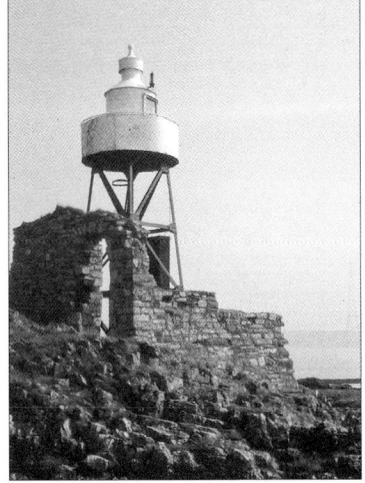

TOUR

Unfortunately to all but those with extensive experience of navigating the treacherous waters of the upper reaches of Bristol Channel with its ferocious tides and currents, viewing the remains should be confined to what can be seen from the shore, preferably with a good pair of binoculars. Even when the tide is out and there appears to be access to the chapel, do not be tempted. Shifting sands, quicksand and numerous other hazards exist and have contributed to several tragic fatalities in this area.

Today from the cliffs at Beachley Point or the (old) Severn Bridge, **the stone arch of the north door (3)** and sections of the **walls (4)** can clearly be seen. The rest of the building is now demolished, possibly as a result of a new navigation light being installed, or crumbled away.

Ordnance Survey Grid reference: Sheet 162 scale 1:50 000: 548901

3 ST JAMES AT LANCAUT

HISTORY

The very early history of one of the most picturesquely located churches in the area, tucked low down amongst fields and woods on the Gloucestershire side of the twisting River Wye and originally dedicated to St Cewydd, has been discussed in the Introduction. It is a grade II listed building, and was a chapel-of-ease attached to Woolaston and then the parish of Tidenham until its deconsecration in 1987.

Curiously the church is not mentioned in Domesday which covers the area in some detail. However, the fact that it possessed one of the six surviving Gloucestershire lead fonts of about 1130 - 40 coupled with the discovery of some finely-carved stones in 1986 point to the existence of a Norman church of some quality, with a rich patron, possibly Walter FitzRichard de Clare who was the founder of Tintern Abbey in 1131 and was Lord of Striguil (Chepstow) in 1115.

It is only in details of the institution of Lancaut's rectors (priests supplied directly by a monastery in return for the parish being attached to the monastery) that one can find any indication of the church's

View of the church of St James at Lancaut before 1880 showing the curious roof structure possibly a bell cote.
Tidenham History Group

history. On July 7th 1297 Roger of Usk was appointed, or *presented* to use the terminology of the time, by his patron Roger Bigod III, Earl of Norfolk, and was the first recorded rector. Unlike many patrons the lord was no absentee landlord, since he had made the castle of Striguil (Chepstow) his home and was busy creating suitable accommodation in the Lower Bailey. He was also looking forward to the completion of his rebuilt abbey church at Tintern where the consecration mass had already taken place.

The new rector must have watched many comings and goings on the busy river where the fishing weirs, such as Walter's Weir and Liveoaks' Trough Weir, often caused obstruction to the passage of shipping. The monks of Tintern seemed to be the chief culprits and the proximity of Lancaut to the Abbey's lands must often have caused friction for the ten tenants of the Lancaut peninsula in 1306. They did not seem to be required to undertake the full scale of labour services demanded of the tenants of nearby Tidenham Manor, but common to all was the additional work needed to support the Earl's campaigns of 1294 and 1295. Rods had to be collected to make hurdles which were shipped to Swansea and oats had to be carried to the army at Newport. Lancaut presented the typical picture of a working mediaeval landscape, so often depicted in manuscript illustrations. On the cliffs above were eyries which supplied the Earl's falcons.

The fourteenth century's patrons came to Chepstow only rarely, preferring to use Norfolk as their base. Thomas of Brotherton, half-brother of unfortunate King Edward II, became the new patron and Earl of Norfolk and Earl Marshal, to be followed by his wife and then his daughter, Margaret Plantagenet, Duchess of Norfolk. They appointed a succession of rectors: Robert of Persfeld (Piercefield), William of Usk, William of Dimmock (Dymock), Robert atte Townsende, Robert of Mesedon, Philip Sherrare and Thomas Jon.

This century brought the calamitous visitation by the bubonic plague known as the Black Death which took a firm grip upon the area in the spring and the summer of 1349. It is thought that a third of the population of Europe died and its effects upon the small community of Lancaut must have been disastrous. There survives in the church what is reputed to be a hollowed-out "plague" stone found near the river, in whose cavity the parishioners are said to have left money immersed in vinegar, as payment for goods delivered by boat.

In 1468 William Herbert, Earl of Pembroke, became the powerful overlord of the large area of land called the March with his base at

Raglan. The patronage of the rectory, however, seems to have shifted to the Bishop of Hereford whose first appointment was William, the Cistercian Abbot of Flaxley. Two years later Thomas Holand appears, followed in 1508 by Sir William Glacier.

In 1518 Sir John Pole of Herleston was appointed rector, springing from the pages of history on account of his somewhat dubious behaviour. In April he was apparently celebrating divine service in the church of Lancaut illegally, having converted the income and profits of the post for his own benefit without licence and authority from the bishops! In July he was still causing offence and in May 1523 he was called to the general court (at Newent) but failed to appear. He was therefore suspended and responsibility passed to the vicar of Wollaston to certify the execution of the mandate of suspension at Monmouth. This was followed up by the vicar of Tuddenham (sic) but Herleston once again failed to appear and was excommunicated. The case was still proceeding in the August of that year, but the outcome is unknown.

A further instance of Sir John's misrule was a case involving a William Henys, a married man, who was accused of adultery with Alice (Carpenter), the wife of William Hopkins of Hewelsfield. A commission to absolve the woman was directed to the Vicar of Tidenham. Sir John's offence seems to have been that he had conducted a clandestine marriage without the required three banns being called. An outcome was that Henys' father, Philip, together with a Robert Morgan, both of Lancaut, laid violent hands on Henry Madocke who had brought the case out into the open.

In 1540 the old Benedictine Abbey church of St Peter at Gloucester became the cathedral of a new diocese, but the patron of Lancaut continued to be the Lord of the Manor of Tidenham, now the Earl of Worcester. William Wellynton, was installed in 1548 by the Chancellor of Gloucester to St James, where it was noted that in 1551 there were nineteen communicants.

In 1560, the second year of Queen Elizabeth's reign, Lancaut was described as a chapel of Lydney and John Pycher was rector, but three years later the post was vacant and there were only five households in the parish. The parish was served by an unlicensed reader in 1576 and there were no sermons or homilies and the statute for church attendance went unobserved. Edmund Arundell, the Vicar of Tidenham, was admitted to serve for a year as rector. Not until 1613 is there any further mention of Lancaut, when the Parish clergy were assessed for the provision of weapons and armour for the militia. In

1629 Joseph Hibb was instituted by or for the Bishop of Gloucester to the *"Rectory and Church of Long Caute."*

Silence then descends and there is no mention of Lancaut until the Civil War when Chepstow's registers record the poignant details of soldiers who died in the skirmish at Lancaut:

"Captain Poors was killed in a battell aft. Lancaute being Governour of Berckley Castle was burried in the Churche of Chepstow the 25th Fetruarie 1644"

"March 15th: William Morgan a souldier of S[i]r John [Wintour] Drowned at Longkate in the battell fought there"

March 16th: A souldier drowned at Longcate in the battle ther".

It is interesting to speculate how the population of Lancaut coped with these times of trouble - and how the church itself featured in the skirmish.

With the Restoration, a Richard Wilkinson has a brief mention as incumbent at Lancaut, to be followed in the same year of 1661 by Richard Bedford, the vicar of Tidenham, who had the curacy. With the so-called "Glorious Revolution" of King William III came the Act of Toleration in 1689 which granted freedom of worship to dissenting groups, but not Catholics or Unitarians. In 1703, in the second year of Queen Anne's reign, Richard Bedford was still the Vicar of both Tidenham and Lancaut, having shepherded his flock through forty-one tumultuous years.

Richard Bell was to be licensed to *"serve the care of souls in the chapel of Lancaut"* in 1708. He stayed for only three years, to be followed by Robert Griffiths in 1711. From this time Lancaut came to be regarded as a chapel to Woolaston and was now under the patronage of the Duke of Beaufort. In 1710 there were four families living in Lancaut. During the 18th century the Church of England continued to be divided between the High and Low Church factions, with the Jacobite uprisings increasing tensions between them but the religious life of many quiet parishes was untouched by the partisanship which raged in the wider world.

Just before Christmas 1737 James Meredith was instituted to the rectory and parish church of Woolaston with the chapels of Alvington and Lancoet (sic) annexed under the patronage of Henry, the 3rd Duke of Beaufort. Seven years later, in June 1744 the Chancellor of the Diocese of Gloucester assigned Woolaston, Alvington and Lancaute into the hands of Somerset Jones, vicar of Tidenham who, a year later, also became the rector of Woolaston. In 1750 a survey of the diocese revealed that only Mr Jones's and Mr Stevens's houses were inhabited in Lancaut parish and that there was a service once a month on the 1st Sunday morning and afternoon alternately, but that no surplices were worn and there was no evidence of the Bible. Nor was there a clerk or a churchwarden until James Meredith had one sworn in during 1738. Later that year J Andrews was ordained deacon and licensed to serve the office of curate in the parish churches of Woolaston and Tidenham. Lancaut was still referred to as a chapel to Woolaston and was worth £14.

In the early years of George III, parsons were rising in the social and cultural scale, living on equal terms with the gentry as never before, but not necessarily in touch with the majority of their parishioners. Sermons, carefully composed, were read from the pulpit as literary exercises, meant to flatter the taste of the squire and his family but were too impersonal to move the patient rustic audience in the body of the church. In 1765 the tithes of Woolaston with Alvington and Lancaut were annexed into the hands of the churchwardens following the death of Somerset Jones until 1769 when Robert Penny MA was instituted.

Even the tourists who passed by on the river failed to notice the little church amongst the trees and it is mentioned in one aristocratic diary as being of only passing interest. The Reverend Penny was an antiquarian whose notes George Ormerod of Sedbury Park later used

Interior of the church of St James, Lancaut circa 1840.
Eleanor Omerod

in his own researches into local history. The growing enthusiasm amongst the gentry for history, architecture and archaeology absorbed many of the more intellectual clergy and scholarship was greatly encouraged by the bishops. In July 1776 Philip Williams was licensed to serve in the parish of Woolaston as curate followed some time later by John Price and Charles Bryan in 1813 who had been presented by Henry, 6th Earl of Beaufort. Ten years later in September 1823 Lelanid Noel MA was stipendiary assistant curate of Woolaston with the chapels of Alvington and Llancaut worth £30.

The history of St James' Church faded as that of St John the Evangelist at Beachley, built in 1833, began. During the 19th century services were only held during the summer months. The adventurous Ormerod family long afterwards remembered one summer service for its holiday atmosphere, the difficulty of access for the congregation, and the pleasant, unusual situation. Eleanor Ormerod, writing of her childhood in the 1830s, recalls it:

"Nevertheless, because of the exceeding picturesqueness of the spot, it was a favourite resort on the twelve Sundays in the year on which (I believe under some legal necessity) service was there, in my time, performed. The scene on the only occasion I was ever present (when our parish church was closed), might have furnished an excellent subject for a painting, as the congregation (far too many for the little church to hold) in their bright Sunday dress, emerged from the sloping glades or woodland, to the open space close by the church. Comfort was a matter of minor importance. Those who disposed themselves on the grass, where they had full enjoyment of the fresh summer air, and heard, through the open door, as much of the service as they chose to- listen to, doubtless enjoyed themselves, but within it was not so agreeable. The squire's family were of course installed in "the Pew" and there we were packed as tightly as could be managed, so that we all had to get up and sit down together. We had a "strange clergyman" reported to be of vast learning; and my juvenile terror, along with my physical condition -from squeezing- has imprinted the morning's performance on my recollection as something truly "wretched".

In 1851 Brunel's South Wales Railway reached Tidenham and in 1853 the Tubular Suspension bridge at Chepstow completed the link into Wales. Thereafter the river trade began to decrease and the isolation and inaccessibility of St James reduced the chances of its survival. In 1853 the growing community at Woodcroft and Tutshill was provided with a new church, St Luke's, and by 1865 the monthly services at Lancaut were discontinued altogether. James William Rymer

The Lancaut lead font at the Marling family home at Stanley Park
Mr A James

was born on 12th June 1865 and christened in the Lancaut font soon after, the last child to be baptised there. That autumn the decision was made to pull down all but the walls of the church.

The bell of was transferred for use at Woolaston School and the font was taken to Lancaut farmhouse, before being reclaimed by the Rector of Woolaston. It then came into the possession of the Lord of the Manor of Tidenham Sir William Marling, who had it restored in 1890, commissioned a new base and placed it on display in his house at Sedbury Park, and later at Stanley Park. The family also added an inscription on the inside rim.

In September 1899 the Rural Dean described the ruined church as being a distinct Rectory in the gift of the Lord of the Manor of Tidenham (Sir William Marling) and valued at £20 net, with only one home in the parish. He also noted that it had contained a Norman leaden font, similar to that at Tidenham, which had been moved by the Patron.

In March 1901 the Vicar of Tidenham and the church-wardens met Mr A W George, estate agent to the Marlings, at Tidenham Church and the hope was expressed on all sides that Sir William Marling would place the Lancaut font at the west end of the north aisle of Tidenham church for the use of the parishioners of Lancaut. This was not achieved, but a letter dated September 1936 indicated a willingness to place it back in Lancaut church if it was ever fully

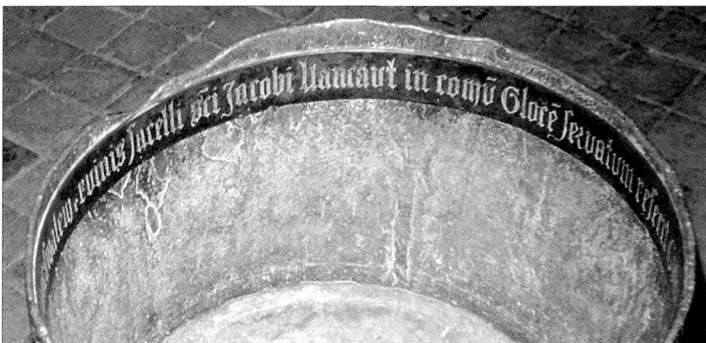

The Lancaut font was inscribed by the Marling family whilst in their safe-keeping. It is now in Gloucester Cathedral.
Liz Pitman

A service held in August 1931 with the choirs of The Chase, Tutshill and Tidenham churches, accompanied by the Tidenham Band and attended by the Tidenham British legion.
Mr A James

restored. The awareness by the Bishop of Gloucester was raised during these discussions and eventually, after the deaths of Sir William and Lady Beatrice Marling, the font was placed in the Lady Chapel at the Cathedral during 1942. The importance of the font is discussed in greater detail in the next chapter.

Despite the official cessation of regular and seasonal services the population of the area continued to hold occasional services at this picturesque church, and an awareness of the importance of the building began to increase. The Gloucester Citizen report on 11 August 1930 stated:

"Many visitors to the Wye Valley are probably unaware that in the area is the smallest inhabited parish in the country- Lancaut, comprising 218 acres, the buildings consisting of the Church (now disused) and two houses, including a farm house, the total number of inhabitants being seven... With the object of creating interest which may eventually lead to the restoration and preservation of this historical church, the Rev.R.P.Steer (Vicar of Tidenham with the Rev. S.G Bush (Rector of Woolaston), held a service there yesterday...Five surpliced choirs from Tidenham, Woolaston,

Alvintgon, Tutshill and Tidenham Chase Churches led the singing, with the help of Tidenham Band....An interesting feature was that the Bible and prayer Book, which bear the dates 1817 and 1799 respectively, and which were used at the Church services, were on view to visitors through the kindness of Mr. E.A. Parker."

A photograph of a service held in the grounds of the roofless church, dated August 1931, shows a large congregation, choir and a band. The notes attached to the photograph assert that an open air service was held annually each year on the Sunday nearest to the 4th August and was attended by the Tidenham British Legion, the choirs from Tutshill, Tidenham and the Chase churches and accompanied by the Tidenham Band. Sadly, the outbreak of the Second World War caused the tradition to lapse, and the little church remained silent for the next 57 years until the next summer service was held.

However Tom Clammer, now Canon Precentor at Salisbury Cathedral, then a young parishioner at the very beginning of his ecclesiastical vocation, described how *" … at 3pm on the 23rd of June 1996, on a beautiful summer Sunday afternoon, a congregation numbering approximately sixty gathered in Lancaut Lane and, after prayers, processed down the steep wooded path to the church of St James. A simple altar and cross were set up against the east wall of the building and once the congregation had gathered within the walls, a service of praise and prayer began. The congregation was mainly gathered from the churches of the parish, but also from the neighbouring Chepstow parish. Tom Clammer led*

Winter 1985 showing the church of St James, Lancaut, at its lowest point of dereliction.
Parry

The interior of St James church Lancaut during the first service held at the church after the second world war on 23rd June 1996 and lead by Tom Clammer.
R Clammer

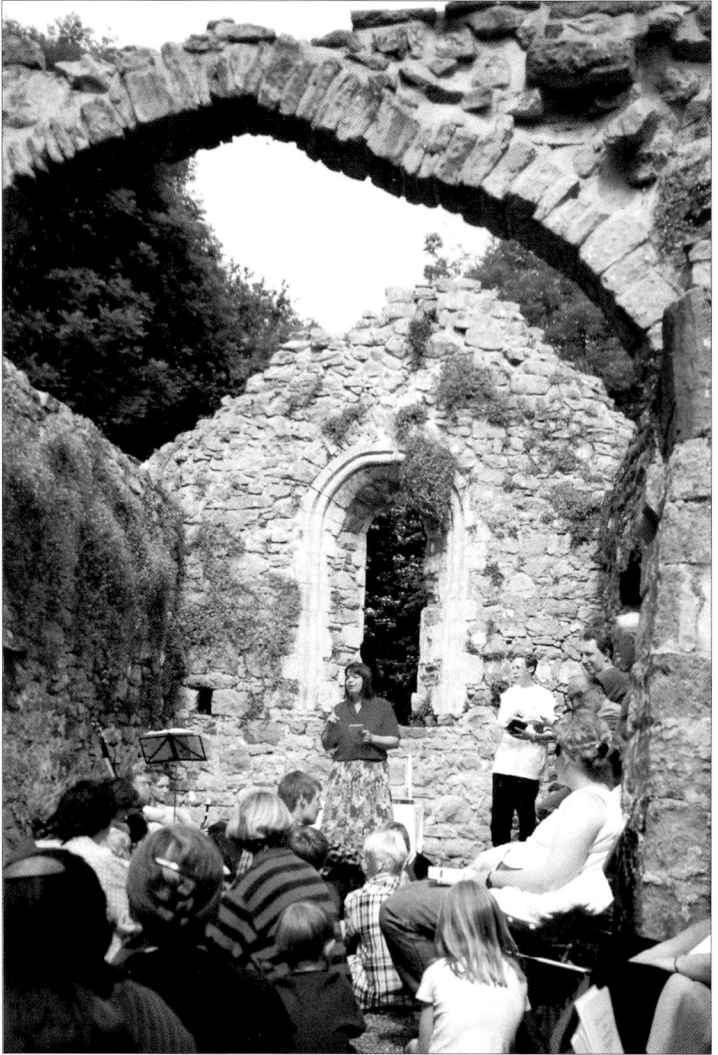

the act of worship, Fiona Gardiner preached, and the Rev Brian Green, the Vicar of Tidenham, gave the blessing. Music was provided by members of the Tutshill Church Music Group. After the service a picnic tea was enjoyed on the grassy slopes of the Wye Valley... It is a testament to the people of the parish, and to the glory of God, that worship continues to be offered on this ancient site, permeated with prayer, on the banks of the Wye."

A service held at
St James church
Lancaut on 6th
July 1997 led by
Fiona Gardiner.
R Clammer

Since that day, two more services have been held on this beautiful site. In 1997 a service was held on 6th July where, once again, Fiona Gardiner preached to a congregation of between 60 and 70. The 1998 service was rained off but in July 1999 the tradition was taken up again as worshippers gathered to attend a quiet meditative service drawing on worship from the Taize and Iona communities.

In 1984, after many years of exposure to the elements, a portion of the chancel arch collapsed and this led to the formation of the Lancaut Church Preservation Group which was absorbed later into the Gloucestershire Heritage Trust who took responsibility for the church from 1987 with some funding from English Heritage. Repairs to the churchyard wall were undertaken in 2010.

In 2013 a group called the Forest of Dean Buildings Preservation Trust negotiated with the Crown to take on St James church as a project and successfully bought the building from the Crown for the princely sum of £1. The Forest of Dean and Wye Valley Review reported in the issue week-ending 13th December 2013 that *"... the chairman Mr Jim Chapman said he hoped the work would begin next summer. Describing St James' as an important and valuable asset, he said its roots were certainly pre-Norman and perhaps even earlier. It is a hugely important building and its isolation is one of its joys."*

THE BUILDING

The Church is of the Norman Period and is 40 feet/13.12 metres long and 12 feet/5.63 metres wide. It consists of a chancel and nave separated by a chancel-arch. There was originally a doorway to both the nave and the chancel but now only that to the nave exists with a large part of the chancel south wall now collapsed. Almost all of the stone used in the construction of the church appears to be local and is mainly of Drybrook Sandstone, possibly from the old quarries on the north of the Lancaut peninsula. Other stone is used in places, for example in the east window and as a quoin, or corner stone, in the north west exterior wall.

The fabric of the nave appears to date from the late 12th century but may be much earlier in origin and the chancel slightly older. A pre-1865 photograph (published in 1904 by Ormerod) shows a wooden structure believed to be a bell-cote, rising above the roof level at the west end. The church bell, possibly 15th century in date, was in situ until the church roof was removed in 1865.

The west gable wall has a two-light opening high up which has been interpreted variously as an opening to house bells and also as a window. The whole building was rendered with white lime-plaster. George Ormerod of Sedbury Park, Tidenham, wrote the earliest accounts of the church, in particular describing the font. His wife and two of his daughters produced drawings and a measured plan.

TOUR

Exterior

One route down to the river side to view the ruins is via a pleasant, if steep descent from Lancaut Lane. Emerging from the trees, the spectacular sight of the roofless church is seen below you, surrounded by a stone wall with a backdrop of the river Wye and huge cliffs behind.

Refer to Fig. 3 for the reference point in this guide. Approach the west end of the church through the gap in the church yard wall where there are two interpretive boards and pause at the base of the **churchyard cross (A)**. The date and form of the cross are unknown.

Look up at the left hand side of the west wall to note a **quoin (B), or corner stone** made of Whitehead Limestone.

There are, high up in the west gable, **two apertures (C)** with holes for possible iron bars. These are not identical, each having slightly differently shaped, roughly pointed arches.

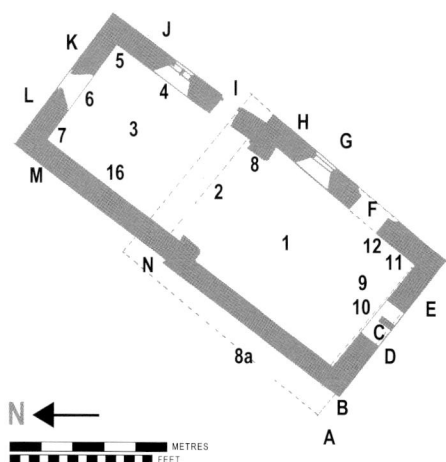

Fig. 3 The church of St James, Lancaut

At the base of the west wall there is a tombstone **(D)**. "HERE LIETH THE BODY OF MARGERARY (sic) WIFE OF JAMES REYNOLDS, DEPT. 1739 AGED 89YRS."

Next to it, again at the base of the wall are the dressed stone **remains of the west chancel arch (E)**.

Moving round to the south side, pass the **door into the nave (F)**. East of the doorway is a **window with iron hinges (G)**. On the ground nearby is another **grave stone (H)** marking the resting place of the son and daughter, Marguet (sic), of James Reynolds both of whom died in July 1741. **The chancel door (I)** is now collapsed and only the lower portions survive. Beyond the collapsed door is a **"put log" hole (J)** in the wall which was where the original building scaffolding was inserted. It is said by some that they were used as lepers' "squints" to enable the unfortunates to observe Mass from outside the church. However, such a squint is said to have been in the north wall of the Chancel within living memory. Moving round the church to the east end there is the **round- headed East Window (K)**. With the exception of one external Red Sandstone block, the double moulded elaborate surround is made of oolitic lime stone probably from the Cotswolds. There are still signs of the glazing bars. On the same east wall is another **put log hole (L) with two more on the north wall (M)**. The north wall of the chancel is **off set** from the nave and this can clearly be seen on the **north wall (N)**. Return to the nave door on the south side, and enter the church to begin the interior tour.

Interior

Once inside the church you are standing in the **nave (1)** the floor of which was paved with tombstones of which some remain to this day. Go through the **chancel archway (2)** and note that the west side collapsed in 1984 but the east side is intact. It consisted of two adjacent arches of unequal height. The intact and slightly pointed eastern arch is formed of small uneven voussoirs, whereas the higher and more pointed western arch was composed of long, quite slender sandstone blocks. It is generally agreed that the arch is a Transitional form (a midway style between Romanesque and Gothic with a constructional date in the late 12th or early 13th century.)

Move into **the chancel (3)** where there is a tombstone to John Stephens dated 1707. On the south wall is a **window (4)** with two lights and three glazing bars. To the left of the window is the cinquefoil headed stone **piscina (5)** having a shallow basin with a drain hole, which held the water for the Holy Communion service. Parry states that it had been dated by some to the 14th century but less specifically as late mediaeval.

The interior of the **east window (6)** shows a single roll moulding. A sketched view of about 1840 shows that this window used to have square window panes and Parry describes how traces of lime-wash covered with red pigments over were visible on the internal mouldings in 1986. The flat sill, having collapsed in 1986 was replaced in 1988.

There was an **aumbrey** on the north wall **(7)** but following repairs nothing remains today. Similarly the altar would have stood in the sanctuary area of the chancel and would have originally had a stone slab with consecration crosses on its surfaces. Many of these were lost during the reformation period. The floor of the chancel was higher, probably by two steps and would have originally had a stone flag floor with some ledger tombstones, one survivor of which has been laid in the gravel that now covers the whole floor are of the church.

Back in the nave, note the **location of the pulpit (8)** on the south wall where the chancel arch support has been cut to accommodate the stairway up. There would have been wooden box pews in the nave on either side of a central aisle facing the pulpit. Also in the nave is the **site of and possible base of the Norman font (9)** which is located by the north wall. The font itself, as described above and in chapter two is now in the Lady Chapel at Gloucester Cathedral.

On the base is what is known locally as the **vinegar stone (10)** of unknown origin. It is locally known to have been sited on the river bank and later moved to the church. It is reputed to be a hollowed-out "plague" stone, in whose cavity the parishioners are said to have left money immersed in vinegar, as payment for goods delivered by boat. Towards the end of the 15th century it is thought that a leper colony was established on the peninsula, the name "Spital Meend" pointing towards a leper hospital.

Nearby is the **gravestone (11)** of Henry Stephen 1682-1748.

Just before you leave this peaceful location note the early 13th century raised **masonry bench (12)** low down and leading from the corner to the nave door.

The church is now consolidated against the elements and will no doubt continue to be the focus of interest for all those who find peace and solitude in this beautiful sanctuary away from the stresses of the world.

Ordnance survey grid reference Sheet 162 1:25000 : 537965

Choirs and clergy snake their way down the hill to one of the annual services held at St James Lancaut on the Sunday nearest to the fourth of August.
Mary Bruton

4   THE LANCAUT AND TIDENHAM FONTS

We have seen in Chapter 3 that the chapel of St James at Lancaut possessed one of the six Gloucestershire lead fonts which is now in the Lady Chapel of Gloucester Cathedral. The parish church of St Peter and St Mary at Tidenham is particularly fortunate in possessing in situ, another one of the six. The others are at Siston, Frampton-on-Severn, Sandhurst and Oxenhall.

Mediaeval churches, particularly those large or significant enough to attract wealthy congregations or having a sacred relic, were enhanced by a range of wooden and stone sculptures, stained glass, altars, screens, fonts and other sacred objects such as reliquaries and candelabra made in a range of metals from gold down to base lead. Even small churches would have been furnished with the necessary items for the priests to carry out the functions of the Church liturgy. Decorations were often bright and highly painted and illustrated biblical themes with the purpose of describing in pictures what could not be read by the largely illiterate population of the time.

The Reformation and the religious turmoil that followed in its wake swept away a vast quantity of these church fittings and only the good fortune or quick wittedness of the priests and laity at the time preserved those survivals we see today. It is known that some fonts were plastered over to conceal their true appearance. Paradoxically it is humble lead which has preserved something of the beauty and style of those lost works. Since it is a commonly used metal which melts at a low temperature, it is even more astonishing that anything has survived at all.

The Gloucestershire fonts may have originated during the period of the third quarter of the 12th Century although some authorities date them from between the years 1130 and 1140. At that time England was the principal lead-producing country in Europe and the mines in the Mendips were the probable source of the material, with Bristol or Gloucester being the most likely centre of manufacture and the river Severn providing the means of transport.

The design of the lead fonts, all made from the same block, is considered to have originated from Mosan Art from the Duchy of

Opposite:
The mid 12th century font from the parish church of St Mary and St Peter, Tidenham.
Liz Pitman

Detail of the font at St Mary and St Peter parish church showing one of the figures of Christ possibly inspired by a detail from the Bury Bible.
Liz Pitman

Lower Lorraine and the Meuse river valley, (Mosa is the latin for Meuse) then part of the German Empire. Lorrainers continued to hold high office in the west of England after the Norman conquest and well into the 12th Century. Three bishops in the west of England were Lorrainers including Walter of Lorraine who was Bishop of Hereford from 1060 until 1079. A troper manuscript had been produced prior to his arrival dating from about 1040 belonging to a house of Augustinian canons of St Victor at either Wigmore or Bristol that is considered to have been a strong influence on the school of enamel-making that existed in the west of England at that time. The manuscript included a trope (or miniature) of St Andrew executed in the Anglo Saxon Winchester style, modified by Mosan Art. Its similarity to the image on the Lancaut and Tidenham fonts is striking.

A psalter, written at Canterbury at the first half of the 11th Century has a figure of St Benedict, which is enriched on the knees in particular with quatrefoils like the trope of St Andrew, a characteristic of enamels rather than miniature painting. It is therefore thought that the maker of the block for the six fonts was possibly an English goldsmith who was practised in enamel work.

The third source is that of the Bury Bible in Corpus Christi College, Cambridge, which was likely to have been executed by Hugh of Bury (1121-48), a prodigiously talented artist who also cast the bronze doors of his own abbey and had a profound influence on manuscript illustration, mural painting and even sculpture. The Bury Bible's design of Christ in Majesty has strong parallels with that of the Gloucester fonts, especially in the seated figure holding the Bible upright on his knee. Both betray the continuing Byzantine tradition in this phase of Romanesque art via Lorraine, especially in the so called "damp fold" of the drapery, intended in manuscript illustration to give the illusion of form to the body It is also certain that the foliate scrolls under the alternate arches resemble manuscript illustrations, for example, in the Winchcombe psalter of the date 1130-1140. It is certain that the fonts were the product of a cultivated patronage during the dominance of the de Clares in this area.

Whichever of these was the dominant influence, it is clear that the arcade and scroll design of the fonts (and a similar stone font at Colehill in Warwickshire) with the impression of applied filigree is based upon Mosan enamels and earlier manuscript paintings.

Walter FitzRichard de Clare Lord of Striguil (Chepstow) from 1115 and his successors during the 12th century, including Gilbert "Strongbow" de Clare, Earl of Pembroke, his son Richard "Strongbow II" who died in 1176 would have been no strangers to travel especially campaigns and pilgrimages and would have been influenced by the designs they had seen.

Detail of painting of Christ in Majesty in the Bury Bible of 1148 which may have inspired the design of the Lancaut and Tidenham fonts. © Corpus Christi College

The interior of Tidenham parish church from the chancel showing the tower screen designed by Sidney Gambier Parry in 1901-2, the font and the ornate choir stalls. *R Clammer*

5 THE CHURCH OF ST MARY AND ST PETER, TIDENHAM

HISTORY

The church of St Mary and St Peter at Tidenham stands imposingly on the hillside overlooking the river Severn. Originally a late 10th or early 11th century church, possibly built at the time when the manor of Tidenham was granted to the Abbey of Bath in 956AD, it was reputedly constructed on the site of a Roman lighthouse. It is thought to have been partially destroyed in the mid 11th century when Gryffed, Lord of South Wales, together with a band of foreign raiders burned Tidenham. The church was actually first mentioned in around 1070 when it was granted to Lire Abbey in France by William FitzOsbern, Earl of Hereford. The manor of Tidenham was forfeited to the crown when William the Conqueror's son, Roger, rebelled against his father in 1075 and was recorded as such later in the 1086 Domesday records.

Because Lire Abbey was too far away to directly appoint its own monastic priest to come and run the services, it was the responsibility of the bishop or patron to ensure that a vicar, (a word then literally meaning *substitute*), was ordained to deliver the religious offices on their behalf. Thus Tidenham was, and remains, a vicarage (a term now commonly used to refer only to the vicar's house). Income from the land and manorial tithes, including parishioners' allocations of goods consisting of corn, hay and wood, or livestock, wool, non-cereal crops, fruit and eggs, was used to pay the vicar. Although by 1291 the tithes were recorded as being granted to two other portions besides the vicar – one probably to Tintern Abbey and the other one to Striguil (Chepstow).

A vicar had been ordained by the early 13th century and in 1289 there are reports that 'the nearby old hall', had fairly extensive farm buildings, including a great grange, dairy, granary, servants' house, and dovecot, indicating a manor of some wealth. In his book *The Forest of Dean*, Arthur O Cooke, refers to the local tradition that the Gloucester Harbour Commission approached the vicar and churchwardens and begged permission for the 13th century tower to be lime-washed in order to serve as a beacon for navigation on the river Severn.

In 1312 Edward II had created his half brother, Thomas de Brotherton, as Earl of Norfolk and the manor continued under that family rule on behalf of the king, exercising the right of the vicar's appointment whilst gaining land, wealth and influence over the local people. Anselm of Leycestra appeared as the first named person in the list of clergy from 1339 but the church living was frequently exchanged in the 14th and early 15th centuries and the parish had at least eight vicars between 1391 and 1395. Henry V took full possession under the Act of 1414 and granted Tidenham to his new foundation, the Priory of Sheen, where it remained until the Dissolution of the monasteries by Henry VIII. Sheen Priory gave thirteen bushels of wheat and thirteen pence to the poor each Maunday Thursday, a practice which continued intermittently until modern times.

Following the abolition of the Marcher Lordships through the Laws in Wales Acts 1535-1542 the parish of Tidenham was transferred to Gloucestershire and in 1570 Francis Shakerley appointed the vicars by virtue of a lease from Sheen Priory. Over the next three hundred years the right of appointment descended with the Tutshill Farm Estate.

Documentary references to Tidenham church in the 16th and 17th centuries tend to relate chiefly to individuals concerning appointments and discipline, patrons and charitable benefactors. The manor of Tidenham passed with the lordship of Striguil, based at Chepstow castle, to the de Clares, and the manor was held by the lords of Chepstow until the 19th century. In 1526 when the inheriting son Henry acquired Tidenham he added the neighbouring manor of Woolaston to it. By 1584 records show the nearby Tidenham manor-house as a building called the Court House which was probably on the same site as the later Tidenham House.

In 1608 the clergy were charged with assessing the population of Tidenham for the provision of weapons for the militia and many familiar local names were listed including Philpot, Madocke, Worwood, Cathmay and Moyle. Three houses at Churchend, near the church, were mentioned in 1614 and in 1681 the church was recorded as having a silver bowl, chalice and a pewter flagon. The Chancellor of the Diocese of Gloucester, as part of a tour recording the whole diocese between 1692 and 1709, noted the following for the parish of Tidenham. The editor John Fendley noted the manuscript (MS) place-name spellings:

"Tydenham.
The body of the church stands upon one rank of pillars. A tower at the west end, 3 bells. No remarkable monuments. …This was an ancient town which Walter and Roger, the brethren of Glibert [MS Gislebert] lord of Clare, wrested out of the Welshmen's hands about 1160.

Hamlets:	1	*Church End*	*12 families*
	2	*Bishton*	*6*
	3	*Sedbury [MS Sudbury]*	*20*
	4	*Beachley [MS Beachly, Bealesly, Bealsly] passage over the Severn*	*20*
	5	*Wibdon*	*10*
	6	*Stroat*	*20*

One and the same constable serves for all. Persons about 700. Families 120 My lord duke of Beaufort lord of the manor. Walding [Waldin] and Beachley 2 manors, belonging to George Lewys Esq."

It is not until the early 18th century that parish records begin and then only sketchily. Although the first register of baptisms, marriages and burials dates from 1708, the register from 1754 to 1793 has been lost. The first surviving volume of churchwarden accounts dates from 1786. There was a vicarage house recorded in 1704. Unfortunately, Somerset Jones the vicar from 1731 to 1769 and also the vicar of Woolaston from 1745, apparently lived at Stroat House and had allowed the vicarage itself to fall into disrepair by 1768, in spite of complaints by the patron James Davis. By 1769 the Duke of Beaufort owned the manor which extended over 2,355 acres and included Day House, Pill House, Sedbury, Tippets, Chapel House farms and 70 acres of woodland, as well as the church itself.

The Reverend Jones was succeeded by William Seys in March 1769, who gained a local reputation as a country sportsman. He was perceived to be the typical parson who enjoyed powerful patronage from the Duke of Beaufort and by his death in 1802 had collected nine parishes including Chepstow and St Arvans, kept a pack of hounds, and did very much what he wanted, including marrying his predecessor's widow. In his later years his son William, who was shy and retiring in sharp contrast to his father, helped as a curate and was reported on bitterly cold mornings when the snow was on the ground as giving each parishioner in the church a couple of shillings to go home and keep warm.

In 1815 under the Act of Inclosure, the parish land was allocated to the vicar, thus making him a significant landowner. Approximately

105 acres of waste land on Tidenham Chase had become glebe (attached to the benefice) and called Parson's Allotment. In addition to this there were the lands of the churchyard, vicarage and adjacent areas, equating to eight acres. There was also approximately 43% of all tithes collected from the rent payable by tenants in the parish. However, G Mead points out in his thesis *The People of Tidenham* that the vicar of Tidenham's living was no sinecure, considering the size and topography of the parish, stating that its income of £450 in 1835 was neither particularly well nor ill-paid compared with other parts of the diocese. However, some incumbants such as Reverends Burr and Morgan had their own personal wealth.

The first surviving Vestry Minute Book starts in 1819 when the screen separating the chancel from the nave was removed. As well as landowning, the vicar was Chairman of the Vestry. Usually nowadays a room usually used primarily for robing and preparation for the service, the vestry was then the room which literally formed the hub of parish administration and in which many parish issues were discussed, most of which were nothing to do with religion except perhaps the costs of upkeep of the church building. Most vicars were also teaching, visiting the poor and sick, and Vestry Minute Books record that they were usually magistrates. Tidenham during the early part of the 19th century did not suffer from the absentee vicar, who left all his work to the curates.

The Vestry minute book 1830-1884 has not survived but key incidents of the time include a request made to the Bishop of Gloucester in 1831 for a house in the village of Beachley to be used as a place of worship by Protestant Dissenters. The Vicar, the Reverend Thomas Thomas, in order to address the threat of competition and to offset any adverse criticism about his ability to retain worshippers, rapidly persuaded James Jenkins a local benefactor to fund a chapel St John at Beachley, as described in Chapter 7. From the early 1840s onwards curates were employed, generally out of the vicar's income, to assist with the increasing amount of parish work, including services held in school rooms.

The Ormerod family worshipped at the parish church, having a box pew which by all accounts was damp and draughty! Many of the vivid illustrated historical documents and descriptions available today are the result of this family's diligent recording. George Ormerod moved into Sedbury Park in 1825, adding other lands to it, including lands in the south part of Sedbury in 1831 and later the Tutshill Farm estate in 1863. The patron by this time was Mary Burr, whose eldest son Daniel Higford Daval Burr succeeded in 1839 and James Burr was later appointed vicar. In the 1840s Tidenham church was used as a week-day school and his daughter Eleanor Ormerod recalls in her autobiography the days when the children would put their bags containing their lunches on the communion table. *"I do not think that this was so shocking "she says" for no irreverence was intended. A table was a table in those days and not an 'altar', and looking back...it does not appear clear where else the food could have been safely placed."* These wealthy landowners in the parish were significant for the fact that it was their patronage, which often enabled changes and repairs to be made to church buildings, parish debts to be reduced or indeed paid off together with other acts of benevolence.

The vicarage at Tidenham was rebuilt by James Burr in 1842 as a stone house with Gothic and Tudor details and gables with decorative bargeboards. On Christmas Day 1844 Mrs H S Burr presented a new altar cloth to the church. On it she had worked in tapestry the representation of Leonardo Da Vinci's "Last Supper". This caused offence to some people when kneeling at the communion rail and they made representation to the bishop. He recommended a meeting to discuss and resolve the matter and accordingly a Vestry meeting was called on 23rd May 1845. However, no one was prepared to protest in public and the meeting recorded that the cloth was *"fully and cordially approved by the undersigned ratepayers and inhabitants [two church wardens and seven others] and no objection was alleged by any present".*

John Armstrong held the living from 1845 to 1854. He was an advocate of the Tractarian or Oxford Movement which looked back to the roots of the Reformation and wished to restore the old ways. The movement was called Ritualistic and its outward manifestations included the encouragement of altar lights, fixed altars, vestments, the sign of the cross, incense and genuflection. Surplices were also introduced for ministers and the choir – an innovation since the minister had hitherto been accustomed to preaching in a black gown. Armstrong's attempts to introduce such measures were not universally popular. The formalising of services, together with his doctrine and style of delivery did not endear him to all. It is possible that this gave rise to Commander Poyntz's decision to build his own chapel at Boughspring, which is described in Chapter 8. Mead's analysis of the numbers of services each vicar performed is revealing; with Armstrong in the lead with four point seven per month whereas the two previous vicars Pulling and Burr and Armstrong's replacement the Reverend Cowburn, averaged three each.

However, Armstrong was respected for his care of the parishioners and his diligence for their welfare. Mead quotes Carter who stated in 1852: *"I remember that we had some bad fevers during the time of my stay there, and his (Armstrong's) remarkably tender affection and excessive anxiety for his children did not in the least lead him, as far as I am aware, to save himself from such visits three times per day."* He became mindful of the needs of the parishioners in the east of the parish in Tidenham Chase and was spurred on, at his own expense, to convert a cottage on his land into a school room where services were held. This, and the subsequent building of St Michael's and All Angels church at Tidenham Chase is described in Chapter 10. Armstrong, unlike his predecessors, had no private income from land or property but wrote numerous religious tracts which generated funds. He used this income to fund the building of Tutshill schoolroom in 1848, which from 1849-53 was used for services and could seat 120, and funded much of the costs of St Luke's church Tutshill in 1853 from his tract writing. He was promoted out of the country to be Bishop of Grahamstown and left in 1854, no doubt to the relief of some of his parishioners.

After a very brief occupancy by Octavious Goodrich, Allan Cowburn was installed as Vicar in April 1854 and lived comfortably in the vicarage with his wife, one daughter and two sons as well as four servants. During his period of incumbency he oversaw the restoration and repair of the parish church drawn up by architect John Norton in 1857. The vicar said that he was in a position *"through the liberality of subscription he had received to complete the work without calling on the parish for further contributions"*. Unfortunately the detailed records for this have been lost but there was an accident reported in May 1858 when a workman on scaffolding *"fell from a fearful height, burying him beneath"*. Fortunately he escaped with cuts and bruises and no broken bones.

A second report in the *Chepstow Advertiser* of August 1858, describes the re-opening of the church on 24th August *"after undergoing extensive alterations and repairs, whereby much greater accommodation will be afforded to the parishioners than in the old structure... After the morning service, a plentiful cold collation was provided in a field adjoining the vicarage; and nearly every family in the parish was presented with one dinner ticket. The creature comforts we understand were provided by the gentry and farmers of the neighbourhood.*

A mid 20th century view of the parish church of St Mary and Peter from the south east side showing its raised rural location in the village of Tidenham.
Eric Wiles

In the evening the Rural Dean preached. Both services were extremely well attended, and collections were made toward defraying the expenses incurred by making the required necessary alterations."

When the Vestry met in 1869 they considered how to raise funds for more church repairs and the celebration of services. It was agreed that funds should be raised by voluntary subscriptions in the parish

An internal view of the parish church, date and artist unknown. Note the elaborate hanging candelabra and the ornate choir stalls. The north aisle appears to show that the box pews have been removed and the vestry created.
Gloucester Archives

and not by a church rate. The following month the meeting was given a list of subscribers and it was resolved that the vicar should visit those not listed as subscribing and explain what was required! The church was again closed for a protracted period for further repairs in the mid 1870s. We do not know the detailed extent of them since no mention is made in either the churchwarden's accounts or the Vestry minute book. A report in the *Chepstow Weekly Advertiser* dated 11th November 1876 reports on the re-opening service after protracted restoration to the roof which cost £1,200 of which £200 was still outstanding. Unfortunately whilst workmen were removing parts of the old roof some of the woodwork gave way and five men fell to the floor. One man, a carpenter named John Poole, died aged fifty-six as a result of his injuries and another one was seriously injured but recovered. The inquest was held at the Tidenham vestry on Saturday 30th October 1876.

With regular services being held in the parish church, St Luke's at Tutshill, and in the school room at Tidenham Chase the need for an additional curate became paramount. In June and July 1886 the *Chepstow Weekly Advertiser* repeatedly ran an advert for a "grand bazaar" to be held to raise funds for employing a curate.

The retired Reverend Feilding Palmer who lived at the elegant house *Eastcliff*, had been voluntarily running services for eighteen years in Tidenham Chase school room to ease the burden on the vicars. The *Advertiser* in its report of July 3 1886 explains that the scheme to raise funds *"having received the cordial approbation of the Bishop of the Diocese, and the support of most of the principal residents of the parish, it was decided to hold a bazaar, the proceeds of which should be devoted to the 'Additional Curate's Aid Society'. The idea, once conceived, was taken up with much spirit by the ladies and gentlemen of the parish and their friends."*

The bazaar was held in the grounds of Tutshill House, owned by Godfrey Seys Esquire, and the patron was her Grace the Duchess of Beaufort. Apparently they were *"abundantly favoured"* by the weather for the two days of the bazaar and at the appointed time on Tuesday June 29th *"a large gathering of the gentry and principal residents of the district assembled to greet her grace"* who, after a welcoming speech by the vicar Reverend J.A.S Hilliard, declared the bazaar open. Amongst those present were Mr and Mrs Seys, the Clay family from Piercefield Park, Mr and Mrs Lowe from Shirenewton Hall, the Marling family from Sedbury Park, Miss Willesford and the Misses Bathurst from Lydney Park, Mrs and

The following amounts have been received or promised:—

	£ s. d.
The Rev. Feilding Palmer, Tidenham	£500 0 0
Mrs. Morgan, Tidenham House	100 0 0
£1000 Stock of the London and St. Katharine Docks Company, given by Miss Churchyard, in 1877, in memory of her late uncle, Henry Churchyard, Esq., value	400 0 0
W. J. Browning, Esq., London	10 10 0
Miss Brown, Tidenham	1 5 5
Mr. E. Butcher	1 12 3
Miss Bird	0 13 0
Miss Churchyard, Tidenham (various gifts)	76 9 7
" " Sale of Fancy Work	60 4 6
" " 187 pairs of Knitted Socks	30 9 2
" " Various Articles	16 18 1
" " Collecting Box	11 7 1
" " Dividends on £1000, London and St. Katharine Docks Co., from June, 1877, to January, 1885	216 5 0
" " Dividends on Donations (invested from time to time as received, in Consols)	71 4 0
Miss Cowburn, Tidenham	3 0 0
Mrs. Fisher, Market Harborough	2 0 0
W. H. Gatty, Esq., Market Harborough	0 10 0
Dr. and Mrs. Goodchild, Hampstead	6 8 0
Miss C. Goodchild, St. John's Wood	3 10 6
Mrs. Grace, London	5 5 0
Henry Grace, Esq., London	3 3 0
Miss M. I. Grace, London	3 3 0
Miss Grace, Tidenham	5 10 0
Mrs. Hannaford, London	0 5 0
Mrs. Hare, Clifton, Bristol	70 0 0
Henry G. Hare, Esq., Clifton, Bristol	22 0 0
S. V. Hare, Esq., Clifton, Bristol	1 0 0
F. C. Hare, Esq., West Kensington	5 0 0
Mrs. Hebert, Silloth, Cumberland	1 0 0

	£ s. d.
Mrs. and Miss Jauette Le Cronier, St. Helier's, Jersey	£7 11 0
Miss Susanne Le Cronier, St. Helier's, Jersey	2 7 0
Miss Moody, Tidenham	4 7 6
Miss C. Moody, Exeter	8 5 0
Mr. Reuben Ravenhill, Staines	2 3 6
Mrs. Rogers, London	0 10 0
W. H. Stone, Esq., and Mrs. Stone, Sydenham	10 10 0
Rev. A. Strong, St. Paul's Rectory, Chippenham	2 2 0
C. W. Wasbrough, Esq., and Mrs. Wasbrough, Abbot's Leigh	5 0 0
Collected by Mrs. Wasbrough, Abbot's Leigh	16 0 0
Mrs. and Misses Whitehurst, Tidenham	1 3 8
Mr. Philip Williams, Tidenham	1 1 0
Small contributions of people of the Chase District	3 15 0
Collected in pence and small sums	5 7 0
Response to advertisement in "Monthly Packet"	0 9 0
May 27th Major & Mrs Cowbran, Tidenham	5 0 0
" Mrs Graham, London	1 1 0
28th The Messes Cowbran, Tidenham	5 5 0
Miss Smith, Dover	1 0 0
Mrs G Foller, Hampstead	1 0 0

The details of the income from the appeal for a new curate including the sale of 187 pairs of knitted socks! *Tidenham History Group*

Miss Evans of Tutshill Lodge, the Gueret family of Castleford House, Captain and Mrs Brett of Caerwood at Netherhope. Others had funded the expense of stalls, including notably Lady Marling, Mrs Seys of Wirewoods Green, Mrs Gueret, and Miss Churchyard of Chase House. Besides these, there was a refreshment stall where "Rebekah (Miss H Hiller arrayed in Eastern costume) waited at the well, and from its pellucid depths from time to time raised the refreshing draught to revive the drooping applicant....Mrs Gueret presided over a collection of snakes and Brazilian beetles...a fine art gallery with Mr Lowe as manager and expositor was on view at intervals during the day... the billiard room had been fitted with a stage, as a miniature theatre and here the renowned Mrs Jarley's 'Animated Waxworks' were exhibited three times a day, Mr Hugh Lowe acting as showman, and afforded infinite amusement."

At the end of the two days, despite the disappointment of the lower than expected turnout on the last evening when the entrance fees were removed entirely (possibly due to the counter attraction of Ginnet's circus in Chepstow) the report concluded that at least £200 profit had been made and *"the bazaar as a whole may be considered to have been a success".*

One poignant newspaper report covered the funeral service of Mrs

Christiana Morgan of Tidenham House, following her death on 11th January 1889 at the age of 71. As will be seen in a later Chapter this lady, described as *"truly a lady bountiful"*, was a significant driving force in the provision of moral, educational and social activities, particularly for people living in the Woodcroft and Stroat areas. Her late husband Thomas Henry Morgan had been a staunch member of the Temperance Society and was a financial supporter of Tidenham churches as well as being a lay member of the clergy. Her oak coffin with silver mountings was borne from nearby Tidenham House and carried without a pall on a bier completely covered with flowers. So large was the attendance that some parishioners could not get into the church. The service was conducted by the vicar, the Reverend J A S Hilliard and a former vicar, the Reverend J S Burd, read a portion of the service at the grave. She was interred in the churchyard and a choir from the Woodcroft Memorial Hall sang at the graveside amidst numerous beautiful wreaths of flowers which had been sent, including one from those who used to attend mothers' meetings which Mrs Morgan held at her house and another from a group of men connected with the Memorial Hall.

The Rural Dean's report on churches and schools dated 24th September 1896 stated that, apart from a few minor points, the parish church was in good repair. However it noted that the communion table was in bad repair and appeared to be falling to pieces. He suggested raising it up as it had a *"very squat appearance from the body of the church."* This was written in the first few months of the incumbency of the Reverend Vincent Charles Reynell, who had been instituted on 10th April 1896 and kept a list of the changes made during his four year period at the back of the Vestry minute book for 1860-1945. Besides structural changes described later including renovation of the bells, it records that the ladies of the parish contributed towards vespers lights, a hanging behind the altar, new hymn books and psalters, new surplices for the boys, a brass alms dish from Mrs Griffiths, and a delicately designed chalice veil worked by Miss Lindam. He also noted that churchyard monuments were straightened and the paths gravelled by the joint voluntary labour of clergy, farmers and workpeople and that the iron stands for candles found in the coal shed were inserted in the finials in their stalls.

The service of re-dedication of the bells at 3pm on Tuesday 20th October 1896 was led by the Archdeacon of Gloucester assisted by past and present clergy of the parish. Additional seats had to be brought

A page from the 1896 Order of Service for the Re-dedication of the Tidenham Bells, listing the costs and work done. Note the variances in spelling, clearly copied directly from the individual invoices. *Tidenham History Group*

O enter then His gates with praise,
Approach with joy His courts unto;
Praise, laud, and bless His Name always,
For it is seemly so to do.

For why? the Lord our God is good;
His mercy is for ever sure;
His truth at all times firmly stood,
And shall from age to age endure.

To Father Son, and Holy Ghost,
The God Whom Heav'n and earth adore,
From men and from the Angel-host
Be praise and glory evermore.   Amen.

The Inscriptions on the Bells are as follows:

The Treble.	John Rudhall fecit 1826, Renovata 1896, J.T. W. M. Rymer, G. Seys, custodibus.
No. 2.	Jeffries & Price, Bristol, 1854.
No. 3.	Jeffries & Price, Bristol, 1854.
No. 4.	God preserve Church and King, W.E. 1763.
No. 5.	Wm. Willett & W. M. Johnson, C. Wardens, 1783.
Tenor.	Charles James, John Maddox, Esqrs. Jo. Smart, Rich. Seaborn, C.W. E.E. 1710.

Tandem labefactam me restituit.
A. M.D.G. et I.H.B.V.M.
Gulielmus H. Marling, Baronettus.
Vincentio C. R. Reynell, A.M., LL.D., Vicario.
Godfreio Seys, Gulielmo M. Rymer, Custodibus, A.D. 1896.
Deum jubilo, festa decoro, vivos voco, mortuos plango.

NOTES.

							£	s	d
Treble.	In the Churchwarden's Accounts of Edw. Prior, for the years 1827, 1828.								
May 29th.	To hawling the new bell from Stroat, and new frame to the Tower, omitted in last Account		-	-	-	-	0	3	0
	To hawling the old bell to the lower yard, Chepstow, Turnpike & attendance						0	4	0
"J.T."	"John Taylor" bellfounders of Loughborough who have recast the Treble and Tenor bells and retuned the others, rehanging them on iron frames.								
No. 2 & 3.	1854.								
Aug. 2.	Chiming bells	-	-	-	-	-	3	0	0
	Paid for recasting two bells	-	-	-	-		26	4	2
	Carriage of bells to & from Bristol	-	-	-	-		0	10	9
	Hauling two bells from Chepstow	-	-	-	-		0	5	0
	William Young's Bill for Repg. Bell Frames and Bell Wheels Stocking Bells and Scarping Beam and Sundry Repairs in the Tower				-		31	0	11
No. 4.	1763-64.								
	Halling the bell to and from Chepstow	-	-	-	-		0	10	0
Dec. 24.	Take in Down the Bell and puting up the Bell	-	-	-	-		0	4	0
May 19.	Paid Mr. Evans for the bell	-	-	-	-		11	11	0
No, 5.	In the disbursements of Willm. Willett, 1784-7.								
	paid for the new bell	-	-	-	-		19	5	6
	paid for puting up the bell and ale	-	-	-	-		0	15	0
	fraight of the bell to Gloucester	-	-	-	-		0	7	6
	fraight of the bell from Bristol to Chepstow	-	-	-	-		0	2	6
	for halling the bell to and from Chepstow	-	-	-	-		0	7	0
	paid for teaking Down the Bell and ale	-	-	-	-		0	5	0
	paid Willm. Meredith for mending the Bell	-	-	-	-		2	12	6
The Tenor.	"E.E." stands for Evan Evans, the Bell Founders at Chepstow.								

A.D.M.G.   Ad majorem Dei gloriam (to the greater glory of God).
I.H.B.V.M.   in honorem Beatæ Virginis Mariæ (in honor of the Blessed Virgin Mary)
There is some doubt whether the Church is dedicated to the Virgin or S. Peter.
The Tenor Bell has 377 vibrations per second.   This may be said to be F. sharp, and the other Bells are tuned to G. sharp, A. sharp, B. natural, C. sharp, D. sharp.   There is no tritone to show exactly in which key the scale is, but it contains the four notes common to the keys of F. sharp & B.
The melody of the tune to the hymn "Lifted safe, &c." is restricted to the notes of the bells, and the tenor note is kept sounding all through.

V. C. REYNELL REYNELL, M.A., LL.D. Vicar.

into the church to cater for the huge turn-out. A letter from the Vicar of Dorchester to the Vicar of Tidenham on 22nd November 1896 acknowledges a request for ornaments for the altar and a letter of 31st March 1897 includes a quotation stating that he had found a set of ornaments : *"As works of art they are considered A1...heavy and massive... If you accept them it is on condition that they are always in use on the altar and if at any time they should cease to be so used, they would be returned to me, so I could present them to another church where they would be in use."* There were details of how to clean the items and a statement that they were to be despatched the following day by passenger train to Tidenham station.

There is a list of completed repairs and restorations in the Vestry minute book for Easter 1902 reflecting the last major works carried out at Tidenham. An account was presented to the meeting and the vicar stated that a sum of about £70 was still required to cover the outlay. Since then the repairs appear to have been of a more limited nature.

Mrs Francis Palmer of Eastcliffe left £1000 in her will on January 1907, to pay the income of the vicar providing he maintain full morning and evening services at St Luke's, Tutshill, each Sunday. In 1910 the right of appointment of a vicar moved to the Bishop of Gloucester, who remains the patron.

In the early 1920s there were complaints about the draughts from holes in the east window. In 1925 it was agreed that the glass, which was a memorial to the Reverend John Armstrong, be replaced. Armstrong's family agreed but suggested that the old glass be kept for a while and it is still stored in the clock room of the tower. Over the years there had been several reports of repairs to the clock and in July 1926 Mr Nolan agreed to give the clock a petrol bath to cure its troubles. However, if more repairs were required, the decision was made that people other than the church should be encouraged to pay as all benefitted from such a visible time-piece.

The Vestry records for 1924-1942 have not survived but after the War the roof of the nave was repaired in 1948 because of dry rot at a cost of £588. The Vestry report also stated that they had received £20 to start a fund for installing electricity which was to act as a war memorial, with a plaque to that effect. The installation was finished in 1949 and the Bishop of Gloucester dedicated it on 25th March that year. According to the 1947 Inventory, the clock was again out of order and two years later at the Parochial Church Council meeting in February 1949, it was reported that the bishop thought it ought to be put in working order again, at an estimated cost of £42.

In 1935 the organ had been described as dilapidated and in 1951 it was overhauled by George Osmond and Co of Taunton, being rededicated in July 1952. Whilst workmen were lowering the ground level of the organ loft floor by fifteen inches in 1951 because of the threat to the organ of dry rot in the floor, seats and the wall, into which the choir stalls were set, they found a six inch gap into a vault and saw several skeletons inside. Vicar Newman, the incumbent from 1935-57, is said to have declared that he knew nothing about them and instructed the work to continue. Thereafter the men apparently backfilled the vault with the soil and the identity of the burials remains a mystery. The workmen also noted the unusual red bricks on the side of the vault, with a very white mortar.

The organ was again overhauled and restored in March 2001 at a cost of about £12,500. The state of the tower had been a constant problem and some repairs were reported as being carried out in 1929 and 1939. In March 2010, during the incumbency of the Reverend

Harvest festival at Tidenham parish church circa 1930. Note the oil lamps throughout the church as well as candles in the sanctuary.
G Webb

Royston Grosvenor, the decision was reluctantly made to stop the church tower clock as necessary repairs to the clock and the steps of the tower were felt to be prohibitively expensive.

In November 2012 the Reverend David Traherne was installed with a widened remit to cover the parishes of Tidenham, St Briavels and Hewelsfield. Discussions are on-going about the possibility of a serious and very expensive restoration project which may be required at St Mary and St Peter's. The parish church is an ancient and beautiful building of considerable historical interest and importance but, as with all historic buildings, time is taking its toll and difficult decisions will once more have to be made just as they have since the Vestry records began in the 18th century. However, the church has great potential and we await the outcomes with interest.

THE BUILDING

Of the first church that stood on the site in the 11th century very little survives. The font is probably one of the most significant features of the later church. One of the six 12th century Gloucestershire lead fonts cast from the same block, six seated apostles alternate with panels of scroll-work in an arcade of twelve Norman arches, Tidenham's font may have originated during the period of the third quarter of the 12th

A stone recording the completion of the Tidenham church's perimeter wall by William Tyler in 1787. The combination of William Johnson's initials (WJ) and his role as the churchwarden's (ch) led to the later local legend that it marked the burial place of a witch, half in and half out of the churchyard.
R Clammer

century although some authorities date them from between the years 1130 and 1140. The influence on the design and the history of these fonts has been described in detail in the previous chapter. The first church then appears to have been re-built in the mid 11th century, after damage from an attack, butthe building which we see today is the result of considerable alteration in the 13th century. The church is heavily buttressed, particularly on the south side, perhaps as a precaution against subsidence on the steep slope.

The layout is a typical two-cell church with nave and chancel

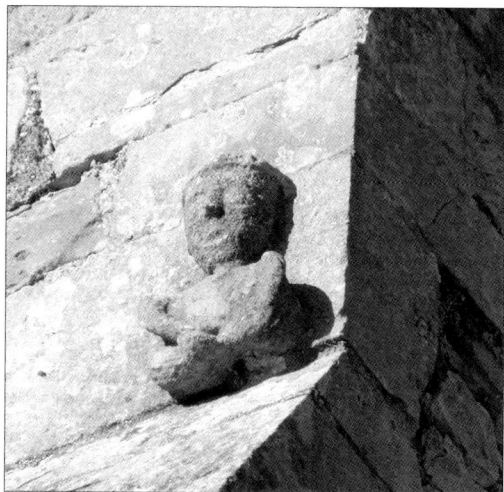

An early figure, one of two, on the south wall of the tower of the parish church at Tidenham. They are possibly from the very early building.
R Clammer

with no separate sanctuary, a south porch, a north aisle, and the early 13th century tower at the west end, the base of which is believed to be the oldest part of the church. The windows in the north aisle are 13th century as is the south door. The church was embellished in the 14th century when windows on the south side were inserted and it still retains some early remnants of mediaeval glass which are illustrated in the colour section of this book and described in the tour and following chapter.

There are some 19th century descriptions of the church from which it is clear that the tower has not always appeared as it does today. Writing in 1803 in his *County of Gloucester*, Rudge notes that the tower was ornamented with pinnacles. Sir Steven Glynn, *Gloucestershire Church Notes* (1830-1874) notes that the east side of the tower was finished in a gable form. The building was white-washed in the mid 18th century, possibly to provide a sea-mark for shipping. During Sey's tenure in 1798 a man was paid ten pounds and ten shillings for "ruff-casting" the church - with seven shillings and four pence for lime and carriage. In the summer of 1819 one pound and three shillings was paid towards the cost of pulling down the partition between the nave and the chancel. On 4th December of the same year a Mrs Briggs was paid for fitting up the vestry room, with the Duke of Beaufort paying for the timber to achieve these alterations.

In 1857 the Vestry meeting considered the plans for a considerable restoration and repair of the church drawn up by architect John Norton. This Victorian period of renovation appears to have resulted in the installation of under-floor heating and a chimney in the north chancel, addition of a porch with a parish room above, creation of two new windows at the east chancel and the west end, adding the north chamber organ, and strengthening the roof. Certainly the date of 1858 on the hopper heads at the top of the down-pipes plus two reports in the *Chepstow Weekly Advertiser* confirm that substantial work was carried out.

A letter in 1883 to Sir Samuel Marling refers to the power given by the Diocese to the churchwardens to remove all of the old box pews, except two at the east end of the north aisle belonging to George Ormerod. In 1883 improvements also included replacing the old cast iron clock and replacing it by one made by Smith & Sons of Clerkenwell.

Of the projects completed during Reverend Reynell's incumbency 1896-1900, perhaps the most noteworthy concerns the bells. In the *Chepstow Weekly Advertiser* dated 24th October 1896 we are told that the bells had been silent for about eighteen months *"during which time they have been in the hands of a firm of bell-founders at Loughborough and have undergone a process of re-tuning and in some cases re-casting; the frame work, which was originally of wood, being replaced by iron and all the mechanism brought up to modern requirement."* The ropes were arranged so that the bells could be rung from the ground floor of the church, instead of from the ringing chamber on the first floor. The church had three bells in 1703 and most bells had been recast or replaced over the years from 1710 as detailed in the Dedication of the Bells service sheet on page 49.

Also during this period the altar re-made with panels loosely inserted after treatment, and the oak table raised on an oak platform. A new roof to the tower was given by Sir W H Marling as were oak gates at both the bottom of the steps and at the west end of the churchyard.

A design for further restoration of the church by architect Mr Gambier Parry, (who had designed St Michael's church at Tidenham Chase in 1888) was obtained at the end of the 19th century and resulted in a screen, designed by H Frith and costing £90 and 14 shillings, being added and placed at the base of the tower in 1901-2. This was one of several items of repair or refurbishment including cleaning and colouring the walls, removal of the font from the tower to the nave and fixing it on a new stone base and platform, and opening a door from the tower to the belfry stairs (allegedly to prevent drunken bell ringers entering and exiting unsupervised). Windows were opened and glazed, resulting in some interesting early 20th century stained glass windows which are described in the tour below and in the following chapter. The steps at the communion rail were widened. The organ was repaired and enlarged but it was not moved to its current location until 1922 when the Vestry applied for a faculty to relocate it to its position in the chancel immediately behind the choir stalls.

In 1955 it was agreed to renew the lych-gate. Finally in 1991 John

Taylor and Company carried out a full inspection of the peal of bells at a cost of £3500 and much work was done by volunteers including Martyn Coles.

THE TOUR

Fig. 4 The parish church of St Mary and St Peter, Tidenham.

A plan of the church and key points of interest (Figure 4) accompanies this tour.

Exterior

The lychgate by R W Paterson was erected in 1955 in memory of Richard Pemberton Steer, vicar of Tidenham from 1914-1930. The perimeter wall of the churchyard was built by William Tyler in 1787 and a stone was originally set in the north wall which recorded Tyler's initials at the top with the date and the initials of the churchwarden, William Johnson, below together with an abbreviation for churchwarden (WJCh). Legend maintains that the locals interpreted the wording on the stone, *witch*, to indicate the burial place of a witch who was buried half in and half out of the graveyard to cover all eventualities! After a period in storage, the stone has now been set into the rebuilt wall to the left of the west gate.

In the churchyard, the **oldest tomb**, enclosed within iron railings, is to the Madocke family from 1587 to 1736 and is located near the main entrance to the church. There are two other early chest tombs to the west which are probably late

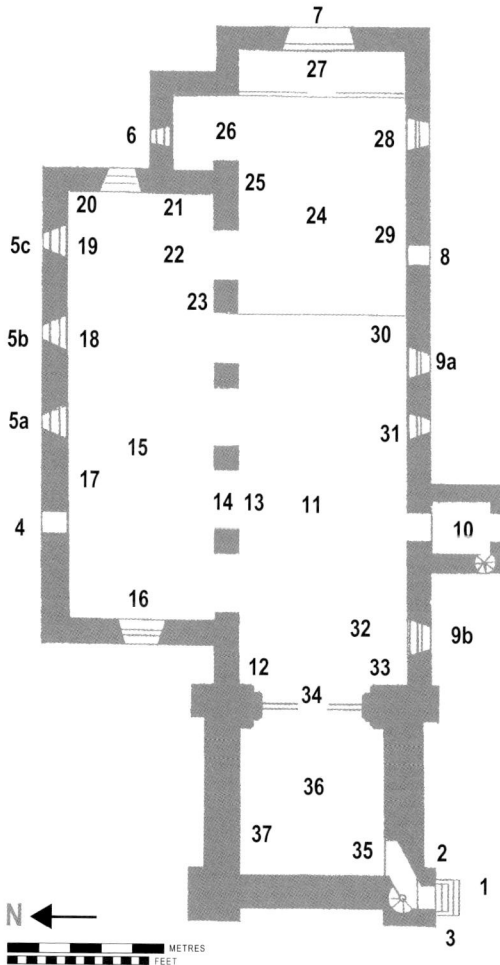

1600s and crisply carved. George Ormerod and his wife Sara are buried in the churchyard.

There are other tombs of interest, with coats of arms or unusual carvings. For example north of the chancel, there is a headstone with a bell on it, in memory of Henry Price, who died in 1910 aged eighty-three. He had been a bell ringer in the church for over sixty years. Another, just to the north-east of the church, is a gravestone to Frank, the infant son of the Reverend John Armstrong, who died aged eighteen days, in 1849.

Starting at the **tower (1)** you will see the different type and size of the stones used in its building. The random rubble construction of the base of the tower is the oldest fabric of the existing church and dates from the 13th century. Looking up the tower you see larger stone block-work below the first string course, and then, between the string courses, there is far smaller stone. The upper stage of the tower is perhaps 15th or early 16th century. The very top is a 19th century addition.

The south west corner of the tower has a simple square turret with external entrance door and small aperture windows. It houses the spiral stone stairs to the belfry. An unusual feature of **two small carved figures (2)** on the tower can be seen at the top of the south east buttress and at approximately the same height on the south-west turret. From their appearance they would seem to date from the earlier church.

There are two types of small lancet windows in the tower. Those in the south are plain and the west stained and it will be seen that from the inside they are very widely splayed. Higher up the belfry windows are larger and of the Perpendicular style of architecture, with brick over the top window on the north side. The larger size of the windows enables the sound of the bells to ring out to the surrounding countryside more clearly.

There is a 19th century cast iron clock on the south face of the tower made in the 1880s by Smith and Sons of Clerkenwell. It has a five foot skeleton cast-iron dial and the mechanism for striking the tenor bell has been disconnected. There is also a weather cock on the top of the tower. There is no west door to the church. The tour continues by going round to the back of the tower and walking along the back of the church. As you approach the corner of the tower, note the Ordnance Survey **Bench mark (3)** low down on the left hand side of the steps leading up to the tower door.

North and South sides

At the back of the church can be seen the original 13th century **door (4)** which with its harsh yellow stone surround (possibly stone from the other side of the Severn) is similar to the east window at St James at Lancaut, even down to the one red sandstone voussoir, or stone block, on the right hand side. A most notable feature is the three **13th century lancet** windows **(5a,b,c)** with trefoil heads in original splays. The windows and doors all have simple chamfered openings with no capitals or mouldings, an unusual feature of some importance in this building.

Further round the church, the triple **window of the organ chamber (6)** made of harsh modern stone can be seen. Inside the church the room is now filled by the organ.

At the **east end (7)** there is little to note from the outside. There is another large clasping buttress, and a stone cross on the gable. The tracery in the window is not original.

Moving to the **south side**, or front of the church, the **south chancel door (8)** has the same stone as the north door and is possibly 13th century. Again, like the north door, there are no pillars or capitals.

There are two particularly fine **windows (9a** and **9b)** to be seen. One, to the west of the south chancel door 9a, is a single ogee window (with a curving double s shaped tracery at the top) whilst the other, to the west of the porch and main entrance door **(10)**, is a double ogee window. As with the chancel door, they have the same continuous carved stone moulding, here following the outline of the window without interruption. They are both rather sophisticated and perhaps the work of someone from Bristol.

The **church porch (10)** was recorded in the Inclosure award in 1815 and was entirely rebuilt in mid-19th century with carved heads and stiff-leaved decorative capitals possibly as part of the 1858-9 renovations. It was plastered and coloured in 1925. Going inside the porch through the Victorian entrance but before entering the church itself, note the very fine late 13th century south **doorway** in the Early English style of architecture facing you. It has later 13th century stone features with slender jamb shafts, rounded with stiff leaf capitals, carving between the upright and the curved stones of the arch, and double-roll bases, unlike the continuous mouldings described previously. It has a well moulded arch with "keel "mouldings, like the keel of a ship in section, used from the late 12th century.

Go through the outer door into the church.

Interior

The inner face of the doorway has stone chamfered continuous mouldings reflecting the earlier 13th century style. Bigland, in his book, *The Historical, Monumental and Genealogical Collection Relative to the County of Gloucestershire,* first published in 1791, notes that the oldest inscription in the church was in the nave to "Grace, wife of William Williams, gent. Died 2nd October 1620".

The furnishings in the church are mostly by Norton in his major restoration of 1857-8. Standing inside the doorway look along **the nave (11)**, or largest part of the church, built for use of the public worshippers. The original pews for the ordinary members of the congregation were not the ones we see today. Indeed in mediaeval times, when the church was built, there would have been no pews at all. Later, they would have been closed pews, varying in size and degrees of comfort. The wealthier households would have had, and paid for, their own pew and there were often disputes when people sat in the "wrong" pew!

One of the main features of the nave is the **lead Norman font (12)** made in the mid to late 12th century and one of six in Gloucestershire cast from the same mould. The design is influenced by Mosan Art that originated in the lower Lorraine area of the then German Empire. The base of the font was made by Norton as part of the refurbishments. More detail about the origins of the design and significance of this font is given in Chapter 4.

Note also the stone protrusions which are **headless carvings (13)** on the north wall of the nave, at the arch junctions and one at the apex of the third arch. They are possibly relics of the destruction carried out at the time of the Reformation or the Civil War.

Look up at the 19th century arch-braced collar beam **roof** which is perhaps a copy of an earlier one. Immediately opposite you is the north aisle added in the late 13th or early 14th centuries, separated from the nave by an **arcade of four pointed arches (14).** These arches are worth noting because, with no decorative mouldings down the length of the piers, they may have been constructed in the 14th century, along with the tower arch.

It is wondered whether there might originally have been a stone arch across the chancel to divide it from the nave. It could have been replaced by the wooden screen which was removed in 1819. It would have been located at the end of the row of pointed arches dividing the nave from the north aisle. Nothing survives except the different planes in the walls between the fourth and fifth arches which are unusual.

North aisle

Moving into the **north aisle (15)**, look up at the trussed rafter roof which is perhaps 14th century and on the south side of the aisle, note the three stone corbels which supported an earlier roof. The **west window (16)** was erected by Thomas Henry Morgan in memory of his father Charles Henry Morgan, the first vicar of Beachley from 1833 to 1852, who died on 13th June 1861 aged 77, and is buried in Abbots Leigh, Somerset. It was made circa 1861 and signed by William Wailes.

Within the aisle we also now see ahead the inside of the **three simple 13th century windows openings (5)**. The glass in the central window is to Thomas Thomas, vicar of Tidenham, 1802-1838. The inscription on the window ledge also includes his wife who died in 1855, and has pretentious claims distantly relating her to Henry VIII!

Of the **list of incumbents (17)** on the north wall of the aisle, David ap Howell (1515-1539) is interesting in that he kept a mistress by whom he had several children. William Seys (1769-1802) was under the patronage of the Duke of Beaufort, had collected nine parishes and kept a pack of hounds. John Armstrong (1845-1802) was a strong supporter of the strict and formal Oxford Movement that met with opposition and probably contributed to him becoming promoted to be Bishop of Grahamstown in South Africa.

There is also the memorial to the **Fallen of the First World War (18)** which dates from 1921 and consists of a marble tablet with a Forest of Dean stone border.

On the same wall can be seen a very small **carving of the heads of an ox and ass (19)** over the manger. This is perhaps a remnant of the Nativity smashed by

Detail of the remaining part of a nativity sculpture probably pre 12th century, depicting the ox and the ass at the manger. The rest of the sculpture was probably destroyed in the Civil War when old glass and monuments were destroyed by Cromwellian troops and there was a Parliamentary garrison at Tidenham.
J Pullinger

A cinque-foiled (five leaved) piscina used during the Holy communion service or Mass. The fifth leaf was cut away, probably to fit in one of the large family pews and the damage was revealed when the pew was removed.
K Underwood

William Lyving, a Parliamentary sympathising vicar between 1539 and 1561. Old glass and monuments were destroyed by Cromwellian troops during the Civil War when there was a Parliamentary garrison at Tidenham.

In the north aisle, behind the **altar made in 1925**, a vestry has been curtained off with a wooden screen, obscuring from immediate view two items of importance. Go into the vestry and in the very far corner of the church where the east and north walls meet note the two square, **glazed putlog holes (20)** where the wooden scaffolding would have been inserted during the original building. They are also similar to those at St James, Lancaut. Were they possibly used as a squint when there was a chapel here?

Returning to the vestry entrance, on the east wall is a cinque-foiled **piscina (21)** although the fifth curve at the front has been cut back flush with the wall. It, too, resembles the one at St James, Lancaut.

According to the Women's Institute *History of Tidenham*, the ancient piscina had been hidden by the panelling of the old box pew which belonged to the owners of Sedbury Park and was revealed when the high boxed pews were removed. The chief parishioners, who sat in these pews hardly had the best position. Eleanor Ormerod, who lived at Sedbury Park, referred to the pews as *"two large, roomy square seats...with a good wall between us and the chancel preventing our seeing what was going on."* With ill-leaded windows to the north and east of the pews *"Sunday devotions in winter were anything but comfortable"*. The Ormerod family used to use the south chancel door as a short cut to their pew. However, one vicar objected to this and removed the latch on the outside of the door. Thereafter Eleanor would take a round ruler to church, insert it through the door, and raise the latch as usual to gain entrance. These old pews were surrendered to the church in 1924 and removed the following year, but perhaps the wooden part of the screen behind the north aisle altar was once part of these old pews.

Before leaving the north aisle and entering the chancel through the more rounded **fifth arch of the arcade (22)** look up once more. It is clearly of a different earlier architectural date and style from the other four pointed arches, appearing to be an earlier 13th century arch because it has chamfered mouldings, as on the outside of the 13th century windows and the inner face of the 13th century south doorway. The stone is also different to that used in the other four arches. Could this once have been the original chancel arch stone re-used? It looks as if it has been rebuilt and certainly isn't architecturally accurate. It was perhaps moved to that position when the north aisle was added. Christie Arno, the architectural historian and expert in mediaeval architecture poses an interesting question and wonders whether the "oldest" looking arch is, in fact, the newest to be built! The rest of the arcade is bald and severe, probably 14th century but possibly very late 13th. The stone of the "new arcade" looks really new, but is not. The stops of the arcade bases are not unlike those of the main late 13th century doorway. The arch is also very crude with fillets (narrow bands), separating semi-circular responds (pillars or piers) attached to the wall to support the arch. Whatever the answer to this conundrum, look very carefully and there are hints of paint remaining in places.

Continuing to look up, the entrance to the **rood loft (23)** survives, above your head and to the right, between the fourth and fifth bays of the arcade.

Chancel

Moving into the **chancel (24)**, including the sanctuary area around the altar, the roof is of original trussed rafter type but strengthened by the insertion of 19th century trusses and curved braces. On the left before the organ you can see what may be the tombed **recess (25)** in the wall behind the choir stalls which was filled in 1951 following observations by workmen of skeletons within, as mentioned in an earlier part of this chapter. The **organ (26)** has been located in various positions and is now located in an extension added possibly as a vestry.

The front of the late 19th century wooden **altar (27)** consists of three carved open-fretwork sections with solid wood panels behind. Similar panels are also at each end. The whole is situated on a carpeted large wooden step. Behind the altar can be seen three stone corbels which were perhaps the support for an earlier altar or a reredos. Behind the altar, the **oak panelled reredos** was made by Jones and Willis and dates from 1905. It was erected in memory of Frederick Mander of Glanynys, Aberdare.

Above the altar the **east window** is an elegant one of three lights with much renewed tracery, described in 1837 as a clumsy copy of Tintern's west window. The stained glass is by Geoffrey Webb and was made in 1925. The central light shows the Blessed Virgin Mary and Child, that to the left is St John the Evangelist, and that to the right St Peter. Refer to Chapter 6 for more information about these windows. This window replaces the original window to the Reverend Armstrong some of which is now in store.

The **chancel south east window (28)** is the first of the existing 14th century windows. It is small with a single ogee ("s" shaped stone carving) and decorated in 1860, probably by Joseph Bell, with a colourful stained glass memorial erected by Thomas Henry Morgan of Tidenham House to Anna Williams, sister of Thomas Williams of Tidenham House and benefactress of the parish who died in 1860, aged 81. There is a brass on the sill to the Morgan family. Nearby is also a **memorial** on the south wall of the chancel to Charles Henry Morgan's wife, Frances Susannah who died in 1831 at the age of forty and to their two daughters, Anna Maria and Frances Harriet.

The **chancel south-west window (29)** contains glass probably made by James Powell & Sons in about 1891. Before leaving the chancel note that the inside of the south chancel **doorway** is an obtuse headed doorway with fine mouldings.

Returning to the nave, by the **pulpit** there is a 15th or early 16th century **window (30)** in which is a stained glass memorial to a former vicar Allan Cowburn (1854-1862). This was also made by Powells in 1892 but it is by a notable Arts and Craft designer, Mary Lownes. (See chapter 6). It portrays the parable of the Good Samaritan. The poor victim must have been abandoned for a long time at the roadside because by the time the Good Samaritan leads him away he has grown a full beard!

Although there is much renewed tracery this window is significant because in the top are fragments of **mediaeval glass from a previous window** to Sir John ap Adam whose manor house was at Badam's Court. He married into the notorious de Gourney family of Beverstone, one of whom was implicated in the murder of Edward II at Berkley Castle. From the left the fragments that can be seen are (i) a roundel of a crown in yellow stain, (ii) two interlocking squares in stain, enclosing the letter "e", (iii) Adam's coat of arms on a shield with five gold stars on a red cross on a white background, and restored inscription "Johes ap Adam mcccx" (1310) and finally (iv) a roundel of a flaming sun which was a Yorkist symbol. This final fragment reflects those who were in power in this area during the Wars of the Roses.

Window (31) is of diamond panes with deeper colour around.

Beyond the door is the **window (32)** constructed with a double ogee, in the 14th century. It contains a memorial glass window to Godfrey Seys, a descendant of Vicar William Seys the vicar of Tidenham from 1769-1802. The window was unveiled on Wednesday January 9th 1907 and is a good example of glass by Butler, Heaton and Bayne of the period. There is a brass plate on the sill below.

To the left of the tower arch is a **memorial (33)** to John Ashley Stafford Hilliard,(1884-1896).

To complete your tour go through to the **tower /ringing chamber (34)**. The arch has two chamfered stone mouldings with double mouldings to the hood mould. The **oak screen** designed by Sidney Gambier Parry under the tower arch was made by the Frith brothers of Gloucester, and added in 1901, possibly to screen the bell-ringers from the congregation.

A tower door from the inside of the tower to the **tower stairs (35)** was opened up and used when, according to the Women's Institute history, there were rumours that the bell-ringers had taken beer into the ringing chamber via the external door, which was thereafter kept locked! When the bells underwent refurbishment in 1896, the ropes were lowered to the ground floor of the tower and the bell-ringers no longer needed to go up a storey to the clock room to ring. In the centre of the current ringing chamber is **a former font base (36)** which was moved there before 1964.

Also in the ringing chamber is a **brass plaque** on the south wall to two families of Belgian refugees who were supported by the parish from 1914 to 1916. Paving the floor are **tombstones** gathered from the floor in other parts of the church. Around the walls are two boards with the Ten Commandments and a board recording Bridget Madocke's charity. There are also some interesting **monuments (37)**. There is a memorial made by Woolcott to Thomas Thomas, vicar of Tidenham, 1802-1838 on the west wall of the ringing chamber. That memorial was erected by the voluntary contribution of parishioners as a mark of esteem for their lamented vicar. Others noted in The Buildings of England are those to Anna Camplin (1812) with a draped urn, by Lancaster of Bristol, and another by Woolcott, for Joseph Camplin (1836) with a broken Ionic column.

Before leaving the ringing chamber, note how widely splayed the lancet windows are on the inside to give more light. The **west lancet window** is by O'Connor and was made around 1858.

Ordnance Survey grid-reference Sheet 162 scale 1:50 000: 556958

The view of St Tecla from Beachley Point showing its remote location from the shore even at low water. *R Clammer*

The church of St James at Lancaut showing the steep path down through the woods and its beautiful rural riverside location on the banks of the river Wye with the precipitous cliffs of Wintour's Leap opposite.
R Clammer

The font at the parish church of St Mary and Peter, Tidenham. This font and the identical Lancaut font at Gloucester cathedral are significant historic items in the parish, dating to the 12th century.
J Pullinger

Tidenham church from the south east showing the east window and the north aisle behind. The later Victorian porch appears to be fairly covered in ivy in this early post card.
Eric Wiles

Tidenham Church, Chepstow.

A 15th century mediaeval stained glass fragment depicting the coat of arms of John Ap Adam on a shield with five gold stars on a red cross on a white background, and restored inscription "Johes ap Adam mcccx" at St Mary and St Peter's church, Tidenham.
Liz Pitman

15th century mediaeval stained glass fragment depicting the roundel of a crown in yellow stain, at St Mary and St Peter's church.
Liz Pitman

A third mediaeval stained glass fragment at the top of a window in the south chancel, depicting the roundel of a flaming sun (a Yorkist symbol in the wars of the Roses) at St Mary and St Peter's church.
Liz Pitman

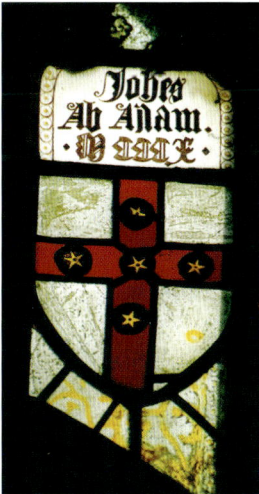

A 15th century mediaeval stained glass fragment depicting two interlocking squares in stain, enclosing the letter "e", at the parish church of St Mary and St Peter, Tidenham. *Liz Pitman*

This view over the River Severn from the parish church of St Mary and St Peter at Tidenham illustrates how valuable the church was as a landmark and beacon to shipping as they negotiated the difficult estuary. *R Clammer*

The base of the tower of St Mary and St Peter's church Tidenham has several significant early C19th memorial tablets and is the ringing chamber for the historic peal of bells. *R Clammer*

In 1892 Arts and Crafts designer Mary Lowndes and stained glass maker James Powell were commissioned to provide a new south east nave window of the parish church of St Mary's and St Peter's depicting the parable of the Good Samaritan. Mediaeval fragments at the top of the original window were left in situ. *Liz Pitman*

Blessed are the dead which die in the Lord

Surely he hath borne our griefs

and carried our sorrows

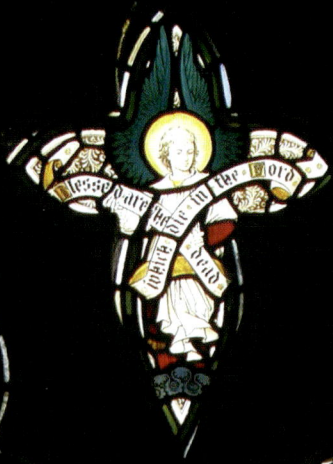

To the glory of God and
John Frank Cyril

in loving memory of
Grace & Ruth Armstrong

The front page of a commemorative book from their appreciative parishioners to Reverend and Mrs Feilding-Palmer on the occasion of their golden wedding showing the parish church and St Luke's church, Tutshill. *Gloucester Archives*

Opposite:
The 1907 window depicting the Marriage at Cana bible story in the church of St Luke, Tutshill. Including no fewer than five portrait heads, it was made by Heaton, Butler, and Bayne and is typical of their strong, figurative style, with clean, bright colours. *R Clammer*

The church of St Luke at Tutshill was built in 1853 to provide an additional Anglican place of worship in addition to the parish church at Tidenham. The architect Woodyer preferred tall pointed features and the bellcote is typical of his work. *R Clammer*

Opposite:
On the west wall
north corner of the
nave in St Luke's
church is a fine
window showing
Christ with young
children. It was
erected in October
1894 "To the glory
of loving memory
of Hilda, Mary,
Mildred and John
Lancelot Lindam".
This window is
signed by
Cakebread,
Robey and Co. of
Stoke Newington,
London.
Liz Pitman

ANGEL OF LOVE

ANGEL OF PEACE

A striking 1907 stained glass window by Heaton, Butler and Bayne in the parish church at Tidenham. *R Clammer*

This detail of one of the children from the Cakebread, Robey and Co. West window of the north aisle at St Luke's church Tutshill shows the quality of detail.
R Clammer

The interior of the chapel of St James at Beachley showing the pulpit and altar and east window. Note the attractive stained glass coloured roundels in the tops of the window reflecting the Gothic style of Foster and Okeley's simple design statement. *Chris Leighton*

The church of St John at Beachley showing the decorative west window and simple west door. *K Underwood*

The south chancel window in St Luke's church Tutshill made by Wailes of Newcastle in 1853. It shows Christ delivering the keys to St Peter and the Redeemer's command to preach the Gospel.
Liz Pitman

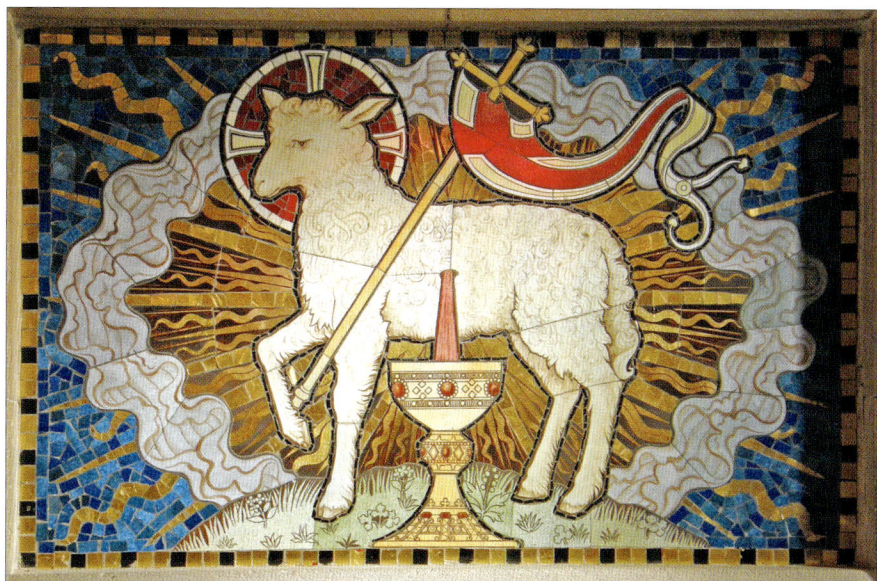

Details of the reredos by Powells in the church of St Michael and All Angels, Tidenham Chase. *R Clammer*

The 1889 east stained glass window of the church of
St Michael and All Angels designed by Gambier Parry
and made by Heaton, Butler and Payne. It depicts an
upper central picture of Christ in the Act of Benediction
with the patron saint of the church
St Michael in the lower section. The side lights show
adoring angels.
R Clammer

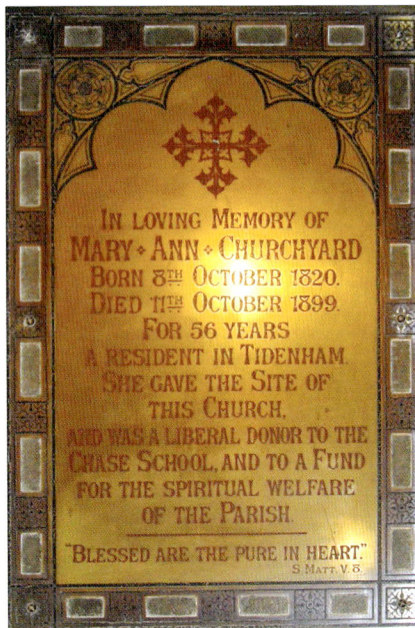

The plaque to Miss Churchyard in The church of
St Michael and All Angels in Tidenham Chase. She
was a significant benefactor and much respected. The
church and community benefitted hugely from her
presence in the area and that of her neice Fanny
Grace.
R Clammer

The striking interior of the chapel of St George in Beachley Barracks, taken in December 2013 with the memorial banner to the fallen from No1 the Rifles Battalion in the centre and the decorative cast ironwork to the Beachley Old Boys' chapel on the left of the picture. *R Clammer*

The interior of St Michael's church in January 2014 showing how the elegantly sparing Gambier Parry architectural style remains fresh, complemented by the striking colours of the altar, reredos and the east window. *R Clammer*

6 STAINED GLASS

The parish is fortunate in having some interesting stained glass which warrants an introduction to help in the appreciation of its workmanship, significance and quality.

It is possible that even the earliest churches had some glass infill in their windows no matter how small the building. Fragments of simple shapes of unpainted glass from the 7th to the 9th centuries have been found during excavations at Jarrow. Early Christian buildings like St Tecla may well have had glass, using the skills from the former Roman presence in the parish, such as Boughspring Villa. St. James and St David-*juxta-pontem* (near the bridge) are likely to have had simple glass, particularly in their chancels. The importance of the royal manor of Tidenham in the Saxon period with its crucial border location, with Offa's dyke, together with the interest shown in the district by King Harold who maintained a garrison nearby, suggests that the early parish church might have had some significant glass. The Abbot of Bath also may have been a possible influence.

Following the Norman Conquest and the establishment of the Norman Marcher lordship of Striguil, the militant Roman Church was most likely to have introduced coloured glass into its churches. The design of the two lead fonts also points to elaborate decoration in the Norman parish church. The influence of the monastery at Tintern however, might have imposed a severe character to the windows, since the Cistercians favoured "grisaille" glass, where restricted colour and abstract shapes were often leaded in serpentine patterns.

Mediaeval glass

It was the belief in the reality of purgatory after death that motivated the feudal magnates and lesser orders beneath them to require the churches they sponsored to recognise their presence, especially in figurative glass. Unhappily the Reformation destroyed much mediaeval glass and only a few 15th century fragments survive in the parish church of St Mary and St Peter at Tidenham in the top lights of James Powell's south east nave window depicting the Good Samaritan. Small though they are, the four fragments from a previous window to Sir

John ap Adam are made using an expensive yellow stain derived from silver and have drawing on them, indicating the wealth of their donor. The photographs in the coloured section of this book highlight the detail of the four fragments: the roundel of a crown in yellow stain; two interlocking squares in stain, enclosing the letter "e"; Adam's coat of arms on a shield with five gold stars on a red cross on a white background below a restored inscription "Johes ap Adam mcccx"; and finally the roundel of a flaming sun (a Yorkist symbol in the wars of the Roses) all combine to give a brief glimpse of a bygone benefactor.

The mediaeval glass maker created his glass by mixing sand, lime and potash which is made from the ashes of plants and seaweed. These three elements were melted together in clay crucibles or pots. The glass produced was called pot metal. Colour was achieved by adding various metallic oxides, such as copper which produced cobalt blue. Coloured pot metal was too opaque to admit much light, so a method was developed called "flashing". Molten coloured glass was dipped into white glass several times before a bubble was blown out. The ends of the bottle, or "muff" shape were cut off and the cylinder opened out longwise to make a sheet. The "flashed" glass was white, with a thin film of colour.

The cartoon, or master design, for the window was laid out on the flat surface and the glass was cut to fit the pattern, using a tool called a grozier to nibble away at the pieces to achieve the desired shape. The glass painters, who ranked highly in the workshop, then painted in the detail onto the coloured background. Once completed the individual pieces were fired to a lower temperature. To assemble the pieces into one window, strips of lead were applied and each junction soldered. Finally a cement-like preparation was rubbed into the crevices to waterproof the window. The completed window was fixed into the window aperture against the horizontal "saddle" bars. Very large windows had additional vertical iron bars, to add strength.

Nineteenth century revival

Although the Gothic style had declined in popularity since around 1600, it never truly died out and circumstances in the early 19th century favoured a revival. As will be seen in later chapters, the Industrial Revolution, including the building of railways, brought a rapid expansion of towns and cities which required new churches for the growing populations. Even rural Tutshill, for example, could be seen as a new suburb of prosperous Chepstow by the end of the century. All denominations expanded, with the Church of England building its churches from the proceeds of parliamentary grants amounting to the then extraordinary sum of one million pounds. Non-conformist denominations, especially the Methodists, built many hundreds of new chapels and, from 1829 Roman Catholics could worship freely, further boosting the need for new churches.

The next earliest glass in the Tidenham parish churches is from the 1830s, a period not noted for excellence, and is in the chapel of St John the Evangelist at Beachley. Here there are coloured roundels at the heads of the lancet windows. (See colour illustration) The windows themselves are filled with diamond-shaped glass quarries characteristic of the Gothic style, giving the interior light and fitting the character of Foster and Okeley's simple design statement.

It was A W Pugin who led the revival in stained glass. His designs recaptured the style of mediaeval work while artist craftsmen like William Wailes revived the mosaic craft techniques of the Middle Ages. A number of illustrated historical studies, published in the 1840s and 1850s, gave craftsmen and designers invaluable information. The most important were by Charles Winston whose studies made him increasingly aware of the short-comings of the glass available to artists of his own day, which was often thin and garish in colour. In 1857 he encouraged experiments designed to rediscover the chemical components of mediaeval glass and persuaded the London firm of James Powell & Sons to make "antique" glass to his recipes. Furthermore, a series of important restorations of mediaeval windows in Bristol and Gloucester cathedrals gave stained glass artists first-hand experience of old glass. By 1860 artists were at last able to obtain glass of a quality matching that of the Middle Ages.

Then follows William Wailes' 1853 east window at St Luke's. Originally an architect, he had set up his studio in Newcastle in 1838. As much a businessman as a glass painter, he was described as a genial man with one of the happiest faces imaginable. His output was vast and by 1851 he was employing seventy-six workers. Unfortunately his west window in St Lukes' was removed in 1929.

In 1858 the lancet window in the tower of St Mary and St Peter's church, Tidenham, was made by Michael and Arthur O'Connor whose work relied more consistently on the bold use of colour. They were also involved with others, such as Clayton and Bell at Highnam church, Woodyer and Gambier Parry's masterpiece near Gloucester.

Joseph Bell's south east chancel window in Tidenham church dates

The east window at the church of St Luke, Tutshill. One of the three original windows made by Wailes in 1853. It depicts the rich designs of the Baptism on the left, the Transfiguration at the top, the crucifixion in the middle and the Ascension of the Redeemer of Mankind on the right.
Liz Pitman

from 1860. He set up his studio in College Green, Bristol in 1840 and was one of the painters who led the revival in the west. He was one of the first to use Charles Winston's "muff" which produced the quality of mediaeval glass.

In 1861 Wailes made another window, this time in St Mary and St Peter's at the west end of the north aisle. Then there was a long pause before the appearance of Clayton and Bell's window in the nave of St Luke's, in 1880. Clayton was an architect draughtsman, sculptor and illustrator. In 1855 he and his partner, Alfred Bell founded their firm, which became one of the most successful and prolific of the Victorian period. In 1889 Heaton, Butler and Bayne made the east window of the new church of St Michael on the Chase that was designed by Thomas Gambier Parry.

In about 1891 James Powell and Sons were asked to make the south west chancel window in the parish church of St. Mary and St Peter. A prestigious London firm, they were encouraged to experiment in antique glass to the recipes of Charles Winston, a significant early pioneer in Victorian stained glass. They specialised in stamped, rolled and pressed glass quarries that introduced textural effects which were cheaper than figurative glass. *Opus sectile* is the name given to a process worked by Messrs Powell & Sons of Whitefriars Glass Works London. It may be described as standing half way between tile painting and stained glass. The material used is an opaque glass of a peculiar nature to which the ingredients appear to be only half vitrified. It is made in slabs of about 7mm or ¼ inch thick, the bulk of the slab being coarse in quality and grey in colour with a thin coating of a finer quality on its surface in a variety of colours. The ingredients of which this glass is made are sifted into moulds in powdered form and fired in a kiln from which they emerge in slab form. These slabs are capable of being cut with a diamond with as much freedom as ordinary glass though requiring a little more care in handling. They are then painted with enamel colours and fired in the glass kiln at a somewhat lower temperature than ordinary glass. Silver stain is used on the whites in the same way as on transparent glass.

The process was largely used by Messrs Powell for reredos and mural monument work in churches, like that of the striking reredos at St Michael and All Angels at Tidenham Chase. As can be seen in the coloured photographs, it figures designs similar in character to stained glass windows, with mostly pale colours and the texture of the surface somewhat similar to that of a coarse egg shell. The pieces were fixed to a wall by means of cement and generally enclosed in a niche or canopy work of marble or alabaster. In design it is much subjected to the same restrictions as regards to outline, shapes of pieces etc. as leaded glass only the outline is not so broad and heavy because unlike with a window, there are no flanges or other impedimenta which require substantial lead-work. It is worth noting that some of the blank panels left by Wren in the interior of St Paul's cathedral were in-filled by Sir William B Richmond from 1891 with glass made by Powells and by Easter 1896 over 10 tons of it had been used!

Arts and Crafts Design

In 1892 Powells commissioned Mary Lowndes to design the south east nave window of the parish church of St Mary's and St Peter's depicting the parable of the Good Samaritan. She was another significant figure

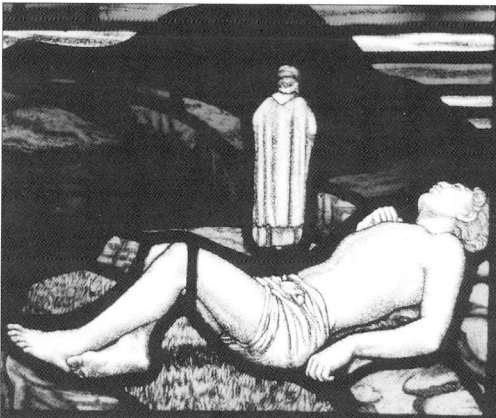

Detail from the window depicting the story of the Good Samaritan at the parish church, Tidenham. *Liz Pitman*

in both the English Arts and Crafts movement but also in the struggle for women's suffrage. She and her partner, Alfred Drury founded the firm in London of Lowndes and Drury which, in 1906, came to be known as The Glass House, a highly influential centre of Arts and Crafts design. In 1894 the west window of the north aisle at St Luke's was made by Cakebread, Robey and Co.

STAINED GLASS **85**

The figure of St Luke from the north aisle of St Luke's church Tutshill was made by Robinson in 1970.
Liz Pitman

Twentieth century glass

In 1907 the south west nave window of St Mary's and St Peter's church depicting the figures of flower bearing angels of Love and Peace, made by Heaton, Butler, and Bayne and is typical of their strong, figurative style, with clean, bright colours as can be seen in the colour photograph in the centre section of this book. Clement Heaton and James Butler had become partners in 1855 and were joined by Bayne in 1862.

In 1925 the east window in the parish church, commemorating the Reverend Armstrong, was removed and replaced by a new one by Geoffrey Webb whose brother Christopher had worked with the architect and stained glass artist, Ninian Comper. They had a preference for late mediaeval and renaissance styles, with lightly modelled painting and pale colours.

In 1970 the lancet window depicting St Luke in the north aisle of St Luke's church, Tutshill was made by Geoffrey Robinson. In 1923 Arnold Robinson had taken over the firm of Joseph Bell and sons, located until not too many years ago at the top of the Bristol Guild building in Park Street, Bristol. He steered the firm away from the effete, refined style it had adopted under George Bell, the grandson of the founder.

This brief outline of the parish glass merely scratches the surface of a fascinating study, but it does show how influential some of the local families were in their commissioning of architects, designers and makers, reflecting their cultural knowledge and ambitions and their contacts with a wider world.

7 THE CHAPEL OF ST JOHN THE EVANGELIST, BEACHLEY

HISTORY

Beachley's significance as a stepping stone on the important river Wye and Severn crossing routes led to the foundation of chapels and probably shrines in earlier days. Indeed the dangers involved in undertaking the passage made the presence of a priest essential, especially in the mediaeval mind. After the desolation that followed the Battles of Beachley in 1644 in the Civil War, when the parliament decreed the destruction of every standing building, there was apparently no place of worship on the peninsular until the early nineteenth century.

It is of particular interest that in the early 19th century the Church of England was due for reform. Despite a liberal movement within the Church, abuses such as pluralism, absenteeism, sinecures and extremes of clerical poverty and wealth went unchallenged and the Vicars of Tidenham were typical of their time. A Whig administration came into office in 1830 with the support of the Dissenters (protestant free-church worshippers who did not want to attend the established Church Of England services). Church of England was already unpopular, the Bishop's Palace at Bristol had already been burned down by mobs and Exeter's had to be garrisoned by coastguards. So it was envisaged that the Anglican church would receive this new government's concentrated attention but it proved to be a moderate one and short lived. It was not until 1835 that it fell to a Tory government under Sir Robert Peel to set in motion a practical reform of the Church.

It was no doubt a significant factor that on June 18th 1831 a request was made to the Bishop of Gloucester by William Williams of Chepstow for a house in Beachley, occupied by a William Luce, to be used as a place of worship by Protestant Dissenters. It was registered by the Bishop's Court on July 7th 1831. Perhaps, in view of Anglican concern for what reforms the new Whig government might introduce, to offset possible criticism and to address the threat of competition from the Dissenters, the Vicar of Tidenham, the Reverend Thomas Thomas did not delay in rapidly approaching the

The view from the Beachley Road of the chapel of St John at Beachley. This route was significant to travellers as it led directly to the newly formed Old Ferry Passage slipway crossing to Bristol across the hazardous river Severn. The school is shown to the right of the church.
R Clammer

wealthiest person in the village to fund a new chapel- of- ease for the community.

On November 10th 1827, James Jenkins and his brother Richard, with others, had set up the Old Ferry Passage Association. Their father, Samuel Jenkins, a maltster of Chepstow, had bought the Beachley Estate from the Lewis family of St. Pierre in about 1790 and in 1801 it was settled on Richard, on his marriage. The Duke of Beaufort, who held the rights of passage from his ancestor John of Gaunt, also had shares in the Company and was a trustee.

An up and coming family such as the Jenkins, who lived at *the big house* Beachley Lodge, would have considered it a priority and their duty as one of the trappings of the new gentry, to increase their prestige in the Anglican community by building such a chapel to serve their family and tenants. After all it was a long way to the nearest church in Tidenham and the passengers on their paddle-steamer the *Worcester*, might also appreciate a place to give thanks after crossing the Severn estuary. It is important to realise that Chepstow and the surrounding district depended heavily on the City of Bristol and deliveries were frequently made via the Severn. The Omerod family at Sedbury Park used landing places at Slime Road Pill in Beachley Bay, but the Jenkins would have used the ferry landing at Beachley.

It was in this climate that James Jenkins largely paid for the new chapel-of-ease and endowed the finance for a Minister's stipend with the dividends from the investment of a £338-19s-8d block of

The interior of the chapel of St John, Beachley showing some of the many monuments to the members of a significant local family and benefactor. It was erected in 1833 and closed in 1998. *Gloucester Diocesan records*

Government stock. This endowment was supplemented with surplice fees and pew rents. At a later date it was also added to from tithe rent charges given up by the Vicar. The church designer and builder were, not surprisingly, from Bristol and it would have seating for one hundred and seventy four people of which one hundred places were free for the poor. The rest, probably box pews, were rented.

The first curate was the Reverend Charles Henry Morgan of Tidenham House. Consecrated on September 10th 1833 by the Bishop of Gloucester, St John the Evangelist was a chapel to the mother

The north transept of the chapel of St John the Evangelist showing the font, the organ and some of the many memorials. *Gloucester Diocesan records*

church at Tidenham. He also consecrated the churchyard for the use of the parishioners for burials. On December 9th 1833 the chapel was licensed for the celebration of marriages.

James Jenkins' brother Richard, whose house Beachley Farm was within sight of the chapel, died the following year in 1834. One might speculate that he may have been in the throes of an illness when the decision was made to build it, as the chapel-of-ease has since become something of a memorial to the Jenkins' family, which will be demonstrated later in this chapter.

By 1841 the population of Beachley numbered some 224 inhabitants in 39 houses. The school had been built adjacent to the chapel in 1840, with an endowment from James Jenkins and there were two inns, the Passage House and the Three Salmons. Thus the chapel served a substantial community. During these years the Anglican Church was experiencing the beginnings of a revival, inspired by both its Evangelical left, and High Church right wings. Between 1845 and 1854 the Vicar was the Reverend John Armstrong who favoured strong Oxford Movement reforms including the wearing of surplices, increased formality in services and challenging sermons. It is not known what the Jenkins family thought about his preaching style but as simple merchants they were likely to have been low-church. Armstrong left the diocese to become the Bishop of Grahamstown in Africa.

In 1847 James Jenkins died and his late brother's son Robert Castle Jenkins inherited the estate, also becoming church warden. Two years later Beachley was established as a Perpetual Curacy within its own parish with a small endowment from James Jenkins and in 1849 the Reverend Canon Charles Henry Morgan of Tidenham House was confirmed in post by the Vicar of Tidenham. The nomination, or appointment, of the curate was transferred to the Bishop of Gloucester in 1865. He died in 1853 leaving the curacy vacant for a year or more owing to the difficulty of finding a curate's house in the parish of Beachley. In 1855 a vicarage was acquired for the curates, a building which is now known as the Old Ferry Inn.

The Old Ferry Passage Association had succumbed during the 1850s after the advent of the railways and particularly with the connection of the South Wales Railway at Chepstow via Brunel's tubular bridge. Boats operated spasmodically, but two tragedies in particular helped to seal the crossing's fate. In her diary Eleanor Ormerod of Sedbury Park noted:

"It was on a stormy Sunday in September 1838, and the boat was heavily laden with horses as well as the passengers. How the accident happened was never known. One of my brothers had been watching the boat from our cliffs, and on looking again, after a minute or two she was gone. The conjectural cause of the disaster was that one of the horses had become unruly."

She commented that it would not be charitable to put the catastrophe down to the fact that the ferry had operated on a Sunday! Fourteen passengers drowned and the only survivor was a dog. On March 1855 a further catastrophe occurred. The sailing vessel "Despatch" was heavily laden after a day of transactions at Chepstow market with twenty sheep, thirty six pigs, five oxen, one horse and a number of passengers on board. A squall threw the vessel onto wooden piles at Aust, with disastrous results. A tombstone in Aust churchyard records that George Pendock and six others were drowned. In St John's churchyard there are graves of children and adults drowned in the Severn but it is not recorded whether or not they were ferry passengers.

With the patronage of the Jenkins family the church's finances seemed secure. There appears to be no reference in the records to the local wealthy Omerod family of Sedbury Park, possibly because they worshipped at Tidenham. A Parish rate had been levied at between two and four pence in the pound. However, in 1868, with the passing of the Compulsory Church Rate Abolition Bill, it was resolved that there should be quarterly sermons preached to obtain funds for the church. Henceforth is seemed customary for patrons to pay off deficits in the church accounts. Ann Castle Jenkins contributed £2-15s-3d in 1870 and the quarterly sermons yielded £8-6s-1d.

In 1875 the Rev. G T B Omerod sold the substantial Sedbury Park Estate and seven hundred and four acres of land to Samuel Stephens Marling of Stanley Park, Stroud who became a baronet in 1882 and had considerable influence in the later life of the church in the 20th century. From about 1880 the names of the church wardens are recorded, introducing some familiar local family names including Joseph Trayhern, James Rymer, Thomas Joyce, Casey Rugman, Henry John Cullimor, Mrs T Prewitt of Beachley Farm, J Pearce, Thomas Peachey Williams and Miss Atkins (who was thanked in the minutes for her services during 1904).

Robert Castle Jenkins died at the age of 89 in 1892 and his son, Richard Palmer Jenkins, became Parish Warden in his stead. In 1893 such was the influence of the family that they had the main road diverted away from Beachley Lodge to increase the family's privacy. Richard died in 1899 and by 1905 his widow, Mary, had married John Matthew Curre, the brother of Sir Edward Curre of Itton Court. In 1906 it was proposed by Mrs Curre that the interior of the church should be restored at her expense and a substantial re-arrangement took place in what had been a compact but crowded interior. The pews, no doubt box pews for which rent was charged, were removed from the transepts and crossing. The whole of the chancel floor was raised to one level and laid with alternating black slate and white stone tiles. The reading desk was removed and replaced by the pulpit. The font, which appears to have been in the centre of the church, was re-located in the south transept, with a drain to the outside. A second vestry or robing room was constructed at the west end. The two stone tablets of the Ten Commandments which had flanked the altar on the east wall were re-located on the west wall. The Curre family had thus made their mark on St John's chapel.

The chapel continued to enjoy a peaceful life throughout the halcyon days of the Edwardian era when people from Chepstow and Tidenham flocked to the area for picnics on Beachley Point and Beachley Bay. The village became a quiet backwater but, as with the rest of a complacent country basking under the sun of the British Empire, this proved to be the calm before the storm that would uproot the whole village.

The government, anxious over the losses sustained by shipping to German submarines in the early years of the First World War, had decided to build two National Shipyards on the Wye. Number 1 was at Chepstow and Number 2 at Beachley. The blow fell in September 1917 when all of the inhabitants including the Curre family of Beachley Lodge were given scarcely eleven days notice to quit their homes and leave the peninsular, initially lodging with family and friends. The school was closed, four cottages near the pier, Beachley Lodge, and the Old Passage House public house were demolished. Eventually two rows of cottages were built for the evicted families, Tubular Cottages near the railway line at Sedbury and Buttington Terrace nearer to Beachley.

The owners of Beachley Lodge leaving their home as part of the evacuation of Beachley Village in September 1916.
The DAILY SKETCH newspaper 17th September 1916

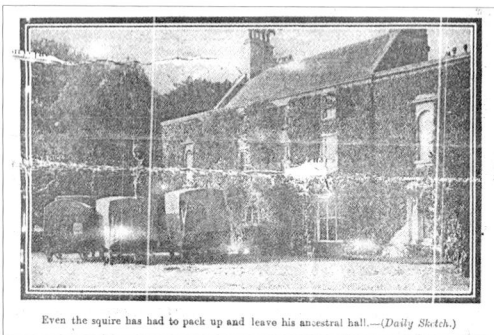

Even the squire has had to pack up and leave his ancestral hall.—(Daily Sketch.)

MONDAY, SEPTEMBER 17, 1917.—Page 7.

ALL THE VILLAGE EVICTED BY GOVERNMENT ORDERS.

Gathering tomatoes in the garden of her cottage home.

Old Richard Traybern, a salmon fisherman, and his crippled wife, will have to leave the pretty cottage they have tenanted for years.

The village sexton and his wife will leave a well-stocked garden.

A population of 6000 Royal Engineers, thousands of shipyard workers and prisoners of war were housed in barracks in Sedbury and Beachley to build the shipyard. At one fell swoop a community was destroyed, and a whole way of life seemed to evaporate, never to properly recover. Ironically, with the end of the war in 1918, the shipyards failed and Shipyard No 2 did not complete a single vessel.

The impact upon the chapel of St John was considerable but parishioners were given permission to come and worship, often under considerable difficulty because of the gargantuan construction developments taking place including the laying down of a substantial railway network. The effect of the upheaval on the Curre family, as well as the death of her husband in 1920, must have been considerable since the minutes record that Mrs Curre was in the parish's prayers and thoughts.

Colonel Percival Scrope Marling VC who lived with his father at Sedbury Park from 1899 and succeeded the baronetcy on his father's death in 1919, became increasingly interested and involved in the affairs of the church of St John and was very active in the parish's support, including financially. Changes had to be made to adapt to the situation and it was hoped to hold services on alternate Sundays. Records show that the insurance cover was raised to £1280 perhaps because of the presence of so many military personnel on the peninsula. Colonel Marling agreed to pay the parish deficit caused by the urgent need to repair the west window, blown in by a gale. There was a further drop in income from collections because of the difficulty in holding regular services. He sold the Sedbury Park estate in 1922, another indication of the changes wrought by the Great War on British society, and left the parish funds with a balance of £12-5s-5d. In 1922 electric light was installed and the church painted. In a determined effort to regain the old normality, a garden fete was planned.

In 1923 the vicar the Reverend R Simmons was recorded as still trying to retrieve the school from the government. In 1924 a new phase was begun when the Army Boy's Technical School arrived from Aldershot to gradually restore order and purpose to a deserted peninsula. Although having several name changes, the institution was to last seventy years and brought an early advantage for the Vicar when the army school padre the Reverend E C Douglas acted as his curate at 6.30pm each Sunday. In 1925 there were fifty-seven communicants at Easter and a sufficient balance of £4-5s-9d to open a bank account. In the next year it was hoped to raise funds for a new organ, since Mrs Curre's legacy could only be used for the sick and needy. A payment was actually recorded in 1927 of £2-11-0d for the sick and needy and an organ was eventually purchased for £10.

A major preoccupation during 1925 and 1926 was in negotiating with the Ministry of Public Buildings and Works for more land to extend the churchyard. A price of £20 was initially refused apparently on the consideration that military burials might be prevented but the matter seems to have been settled by 1927 when a piece of land was arranged for a military cemetery. Civilian burials would be allowed in the extension, but only a few took place.

By 1928 the Army Technical School Padre had given up renting the school house having presumably moved into an army quarter. It was considered that the house could be converted into a home for Mrs Atkins, Beachley's oldest resident. In the next year a large amount of money was spent on repairs so that by 1930 there was a deficit of £1-9s-10d without a patron to write it off! However, parishioners continued to make the journey to Beachley for the services, some of them incurring a substantial walk from Sedbury.

On June 24th 1932 St John's chapel Beachley was incorporated into the parish of Tidenham. Limited services continued to be held but the hey-day of the church was over. In the early days of the Technical School the Padre continued to assist the Vicar and once the technical school workshops were in operation, the apprentices often undertook church repairs and made fittings of good quality. The west window in

The military cemetery adjacent to St John's church was used from the First World War. Graves of British servicemen, their families and apprentices at the Army Apprentices' College are in the foreground and to the left, German prisoners of war are on the right, and the memorial to Italian prisoners of war at the rear.
R Clammer

the form of a wagon wheel or oculus was repaired on more than one occasion, as part of the School's community commitment.

After the Second World War a large number of German and Italian prisoners of war were buried in the military grave yard, and subsequently the Italian Government erected a memorial. One of the most poignant graves is that of sixteen year old Apprentice Tradesman Thornton who was the only person killed in the German air raid on Beachley on November 9th 1940. Another is that of Captain Daybell, of the Wiltshire regiment, who was killed when his cycle crashed into a wall on the Old Hill in the blackout on December 10th 1944. (See tour below).

The church led an uneventful life for its remaining sixty-two years as a place of worship and services continued to be supported by a small but loyal congregation. Perhaps Mary Clist and her mother are perfect examples, being the regular communicant villagers living nearest to the chapel. They lived in what was originally a black tarred bungalow just on the outskirts of Beachley Road and walked to church, along with others still living in Beachley Green. She kept the church bright and spotless until not long before her death in 1966. Margaret Taylor (known as Cissie) was another. She had been a Prickett, one of the old families, and had appeared in one of the many photos accompanying the newspaper accounts of the evictions. Another local person was Mrs Edwards who once kept the post office at the Three Salmons public house, on the road to the ferry. Following the closure of the National Shipyard No 2 and the arrival of the Boys' Technical school she ran it as a boarding house.

With numbers dwindling through age and a possible greater concentration of effort on St Luke's church at Tutshill by the Reverend Brian Green, St John's days were numbered. On June 11th 1994 the final Passing-Out Parade of the re-named Army Apprentices College (previously the Army Technical School) took place on the parade ground within earshot and sight of St John the Evangelist's church. Although the College had from its early days had its own St. George's chapel, as described in a later chapter, links were still maintained with St John's especially for christenings, marriages and funerals. In the seventy years of the army presence its members had become part of Beachley's family and had integrated with the community in the parish, often through marriage. Colonel Peter, perhaps because he felt a pride in living in the grand house that had been Beachley Farm and also possibly subconsciously appreciating that he had in effect become the successor to the previous parish benefactors, the Jenkins, Marling and Curre families, could usually be relied upon to arrange for church repairs and upkeep. He and his Regimental Sergeant Major, were responsible for planting the beech hedge that lines the Beachley Road and for keeping the peninsula landscaped and in order.

In April 1996 the Parochial Church Council and the Vicar agreed that the closure of the church could not be avoided and set in motion the appropriate procedures. The Tidenham Historical Group felt that it had no alternative but to voice its objections along with a good many of the church's congregation. In March 1997, it having been realised that Beachley had been set up as a separate perpetual curacy, moves were made for a merger with Tidenham. It seems that the incorporation in 1932 did not have sufficient standing where a closure of a church was concerned. On August 12th 1997 the Diocese confirmed the proposal and on October 30th the Queen in Counsel agreed but it was not until June 9th 1998 that the Church Commissioners ratified what was called the Pastoral Acheme. This was the date on which the church of St John the Evangelist at Beachley became redundant and the Diocese assumed responsibility for its maintenance as a listed building, pending disposal on the advice of its Redundant Churches Uses Committee. The last service to be held was the funeral of Margaret (Cissie) Taylor in 1998 and then the building was closed.

The communion plate is in the safekeeping of the Vicar of Tidenham. It comprises a cup, probably by R Cattle and J Barber of York, 1811, given by R C Jenkins in 1833. It is a secular piece shaped like a vase, with the sacred monogram IHS (perhaps added later), and embossed foliage with roses, vine leaves and grapes above fluting. There is also a paten, perhaps similar to those designed by Francis Higgins in 1831, a plated flagon and a metal alms dish. Also recorded is a plated metal inkstand presented to the Rev. Canon Morgan in 1852, in recognition of nearly twenty years as minister of the chapel. A plain deal chest of circa 1840 was also once in the chapel, no doubt to house the parish registers.

On April 28th 1999 an extraordinary meeting of the Tidenham Historical Group agreed to the formation of a steering committee to investigate the way ahead and the feasibility of conserving the building. On October 5th the committee called a public meeting in the church which discussed the situation and elected an independent committee to pursue further study. On March 5th 2000 a further public meeting was called, again in the church, which set up a new group called the *Friends of St John's at Beachley*, whose aim was to adapt and conserve the building as a meeting place for small local groups, with the least possible disturbance to its character. The move was welcomed by the diocese and the listed buildings section of the Forest Of Dean District Council. It was felt vital that the Jenkins memorials remained intact in the church and that the architecture of the building should be respected.

During 2000 negotiations were under way with the Diocese for a lease and the Friends were engaging a solicitor and an architect to advise them in the initial stages of what was going to be a challenging project. Several local groups expressed an interest in using the building and support came from many quarters. It would not be an easy ride, but the situation ahead was becoming clearer and plans had been drawn up to make St John's church a centre for the community that, whilst not entirely fulfiling its spiritual needs (religious groups however, had already expressed an interest in using it) would to a certain degree fulfil the Jenkin's original vision of a focus for Beachley.

However, the scheme eventually failed and the Beachley (Army

Apprentices College) Old Boy's Association took a lease on the building, undertaking maintenance and repairs although the Diocese retained their responsibility of this listed building. Eventually The Beachley Old Boys Association withdrew from this commitment and the church has since been used as a furniture restoration workshop. The perimeter wall has been restored and the graveyard and surroundings present a well kept appearance.

Families gradually moved back into the remaining old houses in Beachley, and with the addition of a large number of army quarters for the Apprentices College and subsequent Infantry and Rifle battalions, the population of the peninsula has increased greatly since the two hundred and four souls who lived there in 1841. The modern army chapel of St George (see chapter 12) sits in sharp contrast to that of the Victorian St John The Evangelist.

THE BUILDING

The church of St John The Evangelist is a small cruciform building, faced externally with squared and coursed local limestone and roofed with Welsh slates. See the colour section for further illustrations. It consists of an aisle-less nave, north and south transepts and a chancel. The exterior of the building betrays the partnership's interest in classicism in the pediment-like pitches of the roofs, echoed in the gable ends. In style it is an example

Detail of the bell of St john the Evangelist church, Beachley during renovation of the roof.
K Underwood

The organ of St John the Evangelist in a very sad state of disrepair probably prior to a church renovation, circa 1955.
A T Underwood

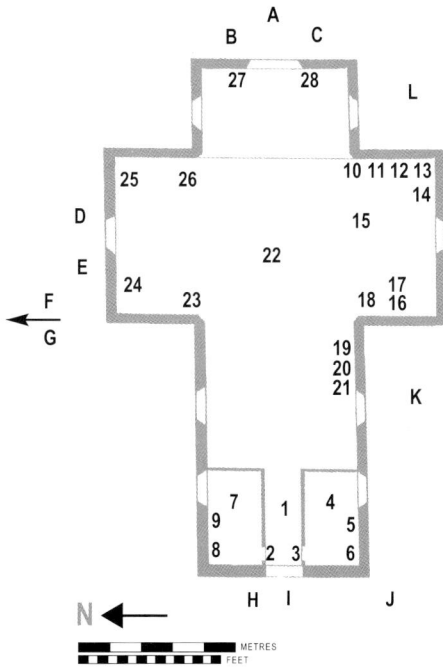

Fig. 5 Chapel of St John the Evangelist, Beachley.

of the Early Gothic Revival and was designed and built by Foster and Okely. James Foster II, who died in 1836, represented the second generation of a family business which produced designs for public and private buildings in the Bristol area from the late eighteenth century through to the beginning of the twentieth century. His father, James Foster I, had been a pupil of the Georgian architect Thomas Paty, who specialised in Gothic. The partnership of James Foster II and William Ignatious Okely designed excellent Greek revival terraces and other buildings in Bristol and a number of Gothic and Neo-Norman churches in Bristol and Gloucestershire

TOUR

The building is used by a private business and therefore is not accessible to the public. However, the churchyards and the exterior of the building are, and it is possible to get a good feel for the church and its proximity to the swiftly flowing river Severn, which has played such a major role in the places of worship in the peninsula. Figure 5 accompanies this tour.

Exterior

At the gate to the church, note the row of cottages to the left and the school house on the right, all reflecting the original village before the turn of the century.

Near the entrance to the grave yard surrounding the church is a **grave stone (A)** marking the death in 1896 by drowning of one of many who perished in the Severn.

The window at the east end (B) is a group of three smaller lancets under linked hoods, with carved, foliate stops.

Below the window is the **grave stone (C)** of Rev. E Green who died in 1905.

Turning to the right, and going round the church in an anti-clockwise fashion, the **windows (D) on the north** are wide, single lancets beneath hood moulds, almost all with un-carved stops.

Looking up at the apex of the west gable is a small **bell-cote (E)**, containing an anonymous bell, clearly bearing the date of the building, 1833. The metal wheel and chain mechanism can also be seen.

Turning to the right, through the entrance to the beautifully maintained war cemetery the **graves of German and Italian prisoners of war (F)** who were originally brought to the area to work on the building of the First World War Shipyard No 2 can be seen, likewise the grave markers from the prisoner- of -War camp at Sedbury during the Second World War. There is a recently erected **war memorial (G)** to the Italians buried here. Since this is also the military cemetery for St George's church at Beachley Barracks, deaths which have occurred in more recent and current conflicts are a reminder of the on-going sacrifices made by Beachley's large and permanent military population.

Leave the military cemetery, return to the church, and walk round to the west end, passing the grave of Enoch Williams who owned and ran the Aust ferry for many years. The **west door (H)** has a simple pointed doorway of great dignity with a **circular window (I)** above it which originally had twelve lights with tracery in the form of a wagon wheel.

At the angles of the building are clasping **buttresses (J)**. In this vicinity of the graveyard are several graves to the **Trahernes (K)**, a Beachley fishing family. Turning once more towards the gate, at the end of the south wall is a large, irregularly formed memorial stone **(L)** behind metal railings to the daughters of Reverend G Bridges who were accidently killed in Jamaica.

Interior

By April 2001, many of the original 1833 features and some from the restoration in 1906 had been removed. The following description, and the accompanying diagram, see figure 5, was written by a member of the Tidenham Historical Group and describes the 2001 internal appearance prior to the building becoming used for another purpose and unavailable to the public.

"Enter the church through the West End door where there is a **crenellated lobby (1)** with an adjacent panelled vestry to the left, both original features. The room to the right of the lobby is an addition from circa 1906. On the west wall, on either side of the wheel window, are two original stone tablets **(2 &3)** within tall narrow surrounds, on which are the ten Commandments.

In the right- hand room **(4)** are two boards **(5&6)** dating from 1833. They read:

ST JOHN'S BEACHLEY

This Chapel was erected in the Year 1833. It contains sittings for one hundred and Seventy Four persons, and in consequence of a grant from the Incorporated Society for promoting the enlargement, building and repairing of churches and chapels, one hundred of that number are hereby declared to be free and un-appropriated sittings for ever.

CHARLES HENRY MORGAN.AM.MINISTER JAMES JENKINS.CHAPEL. WARDEN

BENEFACTIONS

JAMES JENKINS ESQ invested £338.19.8 per cent Consols £ s d in the names of himself and THE REVEREND CHARLES CRAWLEY and Messrs CHARLES SCOTT STOKES and THOMAS HOLT 300.0.0.The dividends to be paid to the Minister of this Chapel for ever...................at the cost of ....

To the left, in the **north vestry (7)** are **three hat pegs (8)** of about 1840. Also in this room until recently was a collection on one board of six panels cut from pew doors and grained as oak, with painted black ovals giving the following names: RD JENKINS SURVR OF CUSTOMS, REV.CH MORGAN, ANN WILLIAMS, JAS JENKINS FERRY PROPRS. Sadly these were stolen when the church was broken into.

In the same room is a **Board (9)** brought from the school room:

THIS BUILDING WAS ERECTED AT THE COST OF ROBERT JENKINS ESQ OF BEACHLEY LODGE & KINDLY PRESENTED TO THE TRUSTEES OF ST JOHN'S CHAPEL IN THIS HAMLET TO BE USED AS A SCHOOL ROOM FOR THE EDUCATION OF THE CHILDREN OF THE POOR, IN THE PRINCIPLES OF THE ESTABLISHED CHURCH FOR EVER.
JANUARY 1ST 1840

Move into the nave of the church.

The church is stone paved in the nave, transepts and crossing, whereas the area surrounding the font has white stone flagstones laid diagonally, with black slate diamonds at the intersections. The raised sanctuary in two steps is laid with black and white marble squares. The open wooden bench pews stand on timber platforms throughout the nave and western sides of the transepts.

St John's main feature, however, is the collection of fourteen monuments to the Jenkin's family which gives the building the appearance of a sepulchral chapel. They are as follows:

MONUMENT (10)

SAMUEL JENKINS ESQ /OF CAIUS COLLEGE, CAMBRIDGE/DIED THE
XXVIII OF MARCH MDCCCXXX IN THE TWENTIETH YEAR OF HIS
AGE/HIS MORTAL REMAINS ARE DEPOSITED/ IN THE RECTORIAL
VAULT OF THE PARISH OF /ST ANN, BLACKFRIARS, LONDON

MONUMENT (11)

SACRED/ TO THE MEMORY OF/ WILLIAM JENKINS ESQr /EIGHTH SON
OF /THE LATE /RICHARD JENKINS ESQr /OF BEACHLEY LODGE /IN THE
COUNTY OF/ GLOUCESTER/ WHO DIED ON THE/24TH JANUARY
1850/AGED 26

MONUMENT (12)

SACRED /TO THE MEMORY OF /CAPTN ROBERT URQUART JENKINS /OF
THE 2ND BENGAL LIGHT CAVALRY /SECOND SON OF R. C. JENKINS
ESQUR OF BEACHLEY/ WHO WAS MORTALLY WOUNDED IN A SORTIE
/FROM THE ENTRENCHMENTS AT CAWNPORE /AND FELL BELOVED
AND LAMENTED /ON THE 26th JUNE 1857 /THREE DAYS BEFORE THE
FINAL SURRENDER /TO THE INFAMOUS NANA SAHIB /BORN ON 24TH
JULY 1828/DIED ON 26TH JUNE 1857

MONUMENT (13)

SACRED TO THE MEMORY OF /SAMUEL RUMSEY JENKINS ESQR/
SEVENTH SON OF THE LATE/RICHARD JENKINS ESQUR /OF BEACH.,
LOD., IN THE C OF G/WHO DIED AT CALCUTTA ON THE 9TH JUNE
1845/AGED 24 YRS

MONUMENT (14)

SACRED/ TO THE MEMORY OF /RICHARD JENKINS ESQ/ OF BEACHLEY
LODGE/ ONE OF HIS MAJESTIES DEPUTY LIEUTENANTS/ FOR THIS
COUNTY /AND MANY YEARS CAPTAIN IN THE /ROYAL MONMOUTH
AND BRECON MILITIA /WHO D AT CLIFTON /THE XIX OF NOVEMBER
MDCCCXXXIV /AGED LIX /AND WAS BURIED AT TIDENHAM/ IN THE
SAME VAULT WITH HIS /THREE DECEASED CHILDREN/ MARY ANN D
XV DEC MDCCCXXI /AGED XIV/DEBORAH D XXI JULY MDCCCXXVIII
/AGED XXIII/ARTHUR SAMUEL D XXI JUNE MDCCCXXXII/AGED XV

ALSO/ TO THE MEMORY OF /MARY NAISH JENKINS/ WIDOW OF THE
ABOVE NAMED/ RJE /WHO D AT B L /ON THE VIII OF JAN/ MDCCCXLVII
/AGED LXVI

Nearby is the **Font (15)**. A tiny stone octagon on a thin octagonal stem,
with a moulded base. The flat oak cover has an iron cross and ring
handle. The date is again probably 1833. It does not appear at all on
the 1833 plan, unless it is the small square at the centre of the crossing,
a compact but unusual arrangement, liturgically speaking.

MONUMENT (16)

IN LOVING MEMORY OF /ROBERT CASTLE JENKINS ESQR FRGS /OF B.
GLOUC./ LATE LXI BNI /SUBSEQUENTLY CAPTAIN /ROYAL GLOU
HUSSARS/ JP FOR COUNTIES OF GLOUC /AND MONM. /B XXVII MARCH
MDCCCIII/D IV OCTR MDCCXCII /BELOVED AND RESPECTED /ALSO OF
/ANNA BASSETT CATHERINE, HIS WIFE/D OF JOHN PALMER OF
CALCUTTA/ B VI MAY MDCCCI / D XXVI NOVR MDCCCLXXXV
ALSO /IN L.M. OF/ RICHARD PALMER JENKINS E /LATE COMMISSIONER
/OF PATNA BENGAL CIVIL. SERVICE /JP FOR THE C OF GLOS /AND
MONMO. /ELDEST SON OF THE LATE /RCJ Es OF B/B XIV JANUARY
MDCCCXXVI/D I OCTOBER MDCCCXCIX

MONUMENT (17)

TO THE MEMORY OF/ MICHAEL HINTON JENKINS ESQr /THIRD S OF
THE LATE R.J.E./ OF B.L./WHO WAS DROWNED WHILST BATHING IN THE
GANGES ON /XXVIII OF JUNE MDCCCXXXV /AGED XXII/THIS
TESTIMONY OF THE AMIABLE QUALITITES /AND MENTAL ENDWMENTS
/FOR WHICH HE WAS ESTEEMED AND BELOVED /BY ALL WHO KNEW
HIM /IS SORROWFULY RAISED UP /BY MATERNAL AFFECTION

MONUMENT (18)

TO THE MEMORY OF /LIEUT.FREDERICK JENKINS /OF H.M. 44TH REGT.
OF FOOT /FOURTH SON OF R.J. ESQ. /WHO D AT KURNAUL IN THE
EAST INDIES /ON THE IX OF SEPTEMBER MDCCCXL /AGED XXV YEARS.
/ENTITLED ONLY TO A SUBALTERN'S PARTY /FOR HIS FUNERAL
OBSEQUIES/ HIS REMAINS WERE FOLLOWED TO THE G/ BY THE
COLONEL /AND EVERY OFFICER AND PRIVATE SOLDIER/ IN THE
REGIMENT.

MONUMENT (19)

SACRED TO THE FONDDLY CHERISHED MEMORY OF /CAROLINE
LETITIA NISBET JENKINS/ A DEVOTED AND AFFECTIONATE WIFE AND
MOTHER WHO DIED/ AT MIRAZAPORE, IN THE BENGAL PRESIDENCY
ON THE 24TH JULY 1848/ AGED 30 YEARS AND 8 MONTHS
"The Lord do so to me, and more also, if aught but death part thee and me". Ruth 1.17.
"Her children arise up and called her blessed her husband also and he praiseth her."
PRO XXI.28.
ALSO TO THE MEMORY OF DECIMUS. JENKINS ESQr /HUSBAND TO THE
ABOVE CAROLINE LETITIA NISBET JENKINS, AND /SIXTH SON OF THE
LATE RICHARD JENKINS ESQr OF BEACHLEY LODGE /WHO DEPARTED
THIS LIFE AT MIRZAPORE, ON THE 21ST JANUARY~ 1857, AGED 37
YEARS.

MONUMENT (20)

SACRED TO THE /MEMORY OF ELIZABETH MARY /AND CAROLINE
MARY /DAUGHTERS OF /DECIMUS. JENKINS AND CAROLINE NESBIT,
HIS WIFE,/ ELIZABETH MARY DIED 29TH AUG 1844/ AGED 6 MONTHS
AND 5 DAYS/ AND INTERRED AT CALCUTTA/CAROLINE MARY DIED
30TH AUGUST 1849/ AGED 13 MONTHS AND 12 DAYS/ AND INTERRED
AT MADRAS/ "TO DIE YOUNG IS BETTER THAN TO SURVIVE
HAPPINESS"

MONUMENT (21)
SACRED TO THE MEMORY OF/ FREDERICK WILLIAM, ELDEST SON OF/
THE LATE DECIMUS JENKINS/ AND CAROLINE LETITIA NISBET, HIS
WIFE /WHO WAS DROWNED AT WESTON-SUPER-MARE /BY THE
UPSETTING OF HIS YACHT /BORN 11TH JULY 1845 /DIED 3 JULY 1867

Before studying the rest of the memorials, look up at the four centred
groin **vaulted ceiling (22)**. It is of plaster and quite successfully
continues the Gothic theme of the lancets, lifting the eye up over the
narrow cornice. The **windows** have plain quarry glazing, with fleur-de-
lys finials. At the head of each light is an attractive, stylised floret of
brightly painted glass. Unfortunately the south west nave windows
have lost the upper parts of their glazing, including the florets. All are
original to this unique William IV chapel. Returning to the memorials
move across the nave to monument 23.

MONUMENT (23)
IN MEMORY OF /CHARLES SCOTT STOKES ESQR/ WHO DIED AT
BEACHLEY/ ON THE XXVI AUGUST /MDCCXXX VII /AGED XLIX /AND
WHOSE MORTAL REMAINS /ARE DEPOSITED/ IN THE BURIAL GROUND
OF THIS CHAPEL.
"AND NOW LORD WHAT WAIT I FOR ?/ MY HOPE IS IN THEE " XXXIX
PSALM 7TH VERSE

MONUMENT (24)
SACRED/ TO THE MEMORY/ ALREADY ENGRAVEN ON MANY HEARTS
OF/ EMMA/ THE BELOVED WIFE OF/ CHARLES SCOTT STOKES/ SECOND
DAUGHTER OF SAMUEL JENKINS/ OF BEACHLEY/ GRANDDAUGHTER
OF SAMUEL JENKINS/ OF CHEPSTOW/ AND SISTER OF SAMUEL
JENKINS/ OF CAIUS COLLEGE, CAMBRIDGE /WITH WHOSE REMAINS
/HER OWN ARE DEPOSITED IN THE/ RECTORIAL VAULT OF/ SAINT
ANNE-S, BLACKFRIARS',LONDON/SHE DIED AT STREATHAM, SURREY
/THE FIRST OF APRIL MDCCCXXXV/ AGED XXXVII /AFTER GIVING
BIRTH TO HER/ SEVENTH CHILD
ALSO OF HER SISTERS/ ANNE ELIZABETH, WIFE OF JAMES NASMYTH
/WHO DIED THE XX OF NOVEMBER MDCCCXXXII /AGED XXXVI /AFTER
GIVING BIRTH TO HER SECOND CHILD/ ALSO DECEASED/ AND
PRISCILLA MILLWARD /WIFE OF THOMAS HUGHES/ WHO DIED THE VII
OF JUNE MDCCCXXXIII/ AGED XXVII /AFTER GIVING BIRTH TO HER
/ONLY CHILD.

MONUMENT (25) This memorial serves as a reminder that wealthy
patrons were invaluable in providing essential funding for this chapel.

In the north aisle is the **pulpit (26)**. It is square in plan, with canted angles, of stained pine in a simple Gothic style, with cast iron Gothic arches at the top of the panels. It dates probably from the church's foundation. From Foster and Oakley's plan of 1833, the Reading Desk stood there, with the Clerk's Desk in front of it, while box pews filled the transepts. It is therefore probably the original pulpit moved across from the south side, assuming that the church was originally fitted out exactly according to the plan.

Move into the chancel area where there is the **Altar (27)**, a strong 1906 oak table in Jacobean style, with turned and gadrooned baluster legs. At the back is a low gradine,(or ledge) of the same period, carved with a vine trail. On it is a dedication plate inscribed "To the Glory of God in Everlasting Memory of my dear Godfather. Given by C N MacDonald." The communion rails, of oak and iron date from around 1890.

Above the altar is the **East window (28)** which has a fleur de lys finial with three typical coloured florets and is original to this unique William IV chapel.

It is rewarding to pause and look up at the windows and the ceiling once more before retracing your steps to the west door. On a bright day particularly, there is a feeling of space and light.

Ordinance Survey grid-reference: 551912

The plaque on wall of the old Wesleyan Methodist chapel, Boughspring. This building was a thriving chapel in the late 19th century and survived until the early 1930s. Many Wesleyan chapels were built in the same modest style as cottages. *R Clammer*

8

THE BOUGHSPRING WESLEYAN CHAPEL AND NETHERHOPE CHAPEL

HISTORY

The Boughspring Wesleyan Chapel

It is unclear how long the alternative houses of worship lasted at Beachley after the Anglican church was built in 1833, but elsewhere in the parish there was a long-lived Wesleyan Chapel, which definitely had a good congregation and survived into the 1930s. The Wesleyan movement was well established and many chapels were being built, particularly in the cities and towns when the chapel at Boughspring was built in 1836. Records indicate that it was registered to a Monmouth minister in 1844 and the chapel had a congregation of around forty-five in 1851.

Nestled into the hill-side in the hamlet of Boughspring, the chapel overlooked the lane and other houses and cottages. Like most buildings of its type the design would have been fairly plain. The Wesleyan Methodist church built a lot of chapels during the nineteenth century and it was thought important to have a record of which they owned or rented and how many they seated. Thornborow describes the latter measurement as being *"...calculated on the basis that Wesleyan bottoms were between 18 and 20 inches wide"*! In the *Returns of Accommodation provided in the Wesleyan Methodist Chapels* in 1873, Boughspring Wesleyan chapel was reported as being in the Bristol District and the Chepstow sub-district which had ten chapels in all and a total number of "sittings" of 1130 of which Boughspring provided 90. The introduction to the report states that whilst there had been a natural focus on the centres of highest population, where enough resources could be found to sustain an independent cause, the Methodist people had been *"quietly but perseveringly continuing their aggressive efforts*

The rural location of the Wesleyan chapel reflects the move in the early 19th century to reach out to rural communities as well as industrial locations.
R Clammer

among village populations, erecting better chapels, and making ampler provision for the spiritual necessities of rural districts."

A later newspaper article in the *Chepstow Weekly Advertiser* on 11th November 1876 reported that: *"On Thursday November 2nd the annual missionary meeting was held at the Wesleyan Chapel, Boughspring, when the chair was occupied and the report read by Rev. W Cumberland. Interesting addresses were given by Rev. W.L.Mayo (Baptist Minister, Chepstow) and Messrs. J King and J Wilson. The proceeds amounted this year to over £9."*

The last Wesleyan report was in 1901 and the Wesleyan movement joined with the Methodist Union in 1932. The actual date of the chapel's closure remains a mystery and the subject of further research. Kelly's Directory for Gloucestershire includes the chapel in the 1931 volume but by 1935 there is no mention of it. Local residents recall the chapel being used for a time as a church boys' club. Then, contrary to some records it was not totally demolished but converted into a house during the 1960s. The current owner described seeing evidence of the original walls, built with lime-mortar, at the roof space level and the quoins (corner- stones) are visible on the lower portions of the original building. Please note this building is a private house and respect the privacy of the owners.

Netherhope Chapel

On Netherhope Lane there is a building which has the regularly spaced arched window features of a chapel. A Tidenham resident described how her great, great grandfather Commander Newdigate Poyntz, a retired Royal Navy captain living at Netherhope House, set out to build an alternative place of worship in the mid 1840s. Born in 1785, he moved to the area after retiring from the navy, bought Netherhope House and promptly built a watch tower in the garden to enable him to following the shipping movements in the Severn estuary. He then started to build another property nearby called Caerwood, which is still lived in by a descendant of the family. He later also bought Ashberry House. His son, also named Newdigate, entrusted Ashberry to his spinster daughters on his death.

His reasoning for building the chapel is not documented but the family believe that he was unhappy with the vicar of Tidenham. During the 1840s there were three vicars, the Reverends Pulling (1839-42), Burr (1842-45) and Armstrong (1845-54). The latter, as has been described in Chapter 5, was an ardent supporter of the Oxford

The mysterious chapel-like building at Netherhope at the beginning of the restoration process. No records exist within the family of the original owner's intentions for this building and for many years it was the home of two families.
Mrs S J Gilchrist

Movement which sought to formalise the services and encourage worship. He wrote and sold religious Tracts, using the funding for his many good works in the parish, and also to support houses for rehabilitating "fallen women" in London. His preaching style was not to everyone's taste and Commander Poyntz, a practising Anglican, whose father had been a rector at Tormarten, and one of whose sons later went on to become a rector at Shrewsbury, clearly found his patience stretched to the limits and decided to provide his own place of worship.

Sadly no designs or plans for the chapel exist. However, the size of the building indicates that this was probably too large for a family chapel alone. Bearing in mind that at the time the only other alternative within the parish was St John's at Beachley run by the curate Reverend Morgan, Commander Poyntz may well have anticipated that the three family homes plus servants and other local people in

Work begins on the interior of the Netherhope building. Note the considerable height.
Mrs S J Gilchrist

Netherhope, Tidenham, Boughspring and the surrounding area may well have filled the pews. Unfortunately Commander Poyntz died in 1853 aged sixty-eight, before the chapel was completed and only one year before Reverend Armstrong was rather suddenly promoted out of the parish to a posting overseas as Bishop of Grahamstown in South Africa.

The building led a chequered life thereafter. It was possibly used at one time as a laundry, although the family point out that there was no water nearer than the well at Netherhope House. It was definitely converted into two cottages and during a recent renovation sheets of newspapers dating to the late 1880s were revealed, being used as lining paper beneath layers of wallpaper. Over the years the two cottages continued to be occupied by tenants until the 1950s when one of the cottages was condemned and the other was occupied until the 1980s after which nature began to take over the site. Then in 1997 a decision was made by a member of the family to renovate the building and create a single house which retained as many of the external original features as possible.

It appears to have had an east/west traditional alignment with a central door on the south side. Whether by original design or as a result of a later conversion, there is a door located under both the east and

west windows. The windows are arched and plain giving good light and the roof sufficiently high to present the possibility that there may have been plans for a gallery. During the last renovation the interior was stripped out completely revealing the size of the original building as a chapel which could certainly have seated well over fifty people and possibly more in a gallery.

The chapel remains something of a mystery. What is clear is that the family members living in Caerwood continued to support Tidenham church. Captain Spencer Brett RN and Mrs Brett (neé Poyntz), of Caerwood, feature in the 1886 summer fund-raising for a second curate to assist the vicar and later, in September 1886, Captain Spencer Brett RN presented a leaving address to the Tutshill curate the Reverend Sale on behalf of the vicar who was unable to attend. In reply Captain Brett was commended and thanked for "the great work" that he had done for the parish. Vestry records also exist of Reverend Poyntz purchasing altar-ware for the parish church in 1897 in memory of his parents who were buried in the churchyard.

Please note that this is a private house and respect the privacy of the owners.

A pre-1896 view of the church of St Luke at Tutshill, consecrated in 1853.
Gloucester Archives

9 THE CHURCH OF ST LUKE, TUTSHILL

HISTORY

By the early nineteenth century Chepstow was a prosperous market town and port with strong links with Bristol and Bath. The Inclosure Acts of the eighteenth century had brought much of the common land into the hands of the gentry whose overlord was the Duke of Beaufort. Speculation began in 1828 with the selling of building plots for Victorian villas in the Gloucester Road district of Tutshill during the 40s and 50s. The Wye tours had already opened up the Wye valley to the early tourists on the Picturesque trail and Tutshill, overlooking the Wye Gorge, provided an ideal location. Communications improved with the turnpike acts and the first steam packet between Bristol and Chepstow started sailing in 1822, cutting travelling time appreciably. The Old Passage Ferry at Beachley was established in the 1830s, Brunel's South Wales Railway arrived on June 18th 1850 and the line across the river to Chepstow by April 18th 1853. The need for a new church to serve the increasing population of Tutshill was evident.

In 1849 the schoolroom had been licensed for religious services but the space was insufficient for the growing congregation, so a former vicar of the parish, the Reverend J.H.S Burr, who owned the field adjoining the school selected that as the site for St Luke's church in March 1852. It was situated adjacent to the Coleford Road between Oakfield Villa and the school.

The plans, with a design by prestigious architect Henry Woodyer at an estimated cost of £945, were approved by the Gloucester Diocesan Church Building Society on the 8th June 1852. The cost of the chancel part of the building was given by Higford Burr Esq., patron of the living. On the date of approval a large assembly gathered near the spot designated for the chancel for the laying of the first stone which was suspended by a triangular frame over which fluttered the Union flag. About two hundred children from the three schools in the parish gathered in the school house and then joined the procession headed by the church wardens, the vicar the Reverend John Armstrong, the curate the Reverend J Brooks and other clergy from the parishes in the area, all in surplices and hoods and followed by the church choir.

The Consecration of St Luke's Church took place on August 12th 1853. Early on a fine morning the parishioners made their way to the church, to the accompaniment of church bells of St Mary and St. Peter, Tidenham. The gate into the burial ground adjacent to the church was decorated by an arch of ever-green branches, flowers, small banners and flags with the name of the church and the district in which it stood. School children lined each side of the path leading to the south porch.

The ceremony was performed by the Lord Bishop of Gloucester and Bristol, who was met at the School House by forty robed clergymen who then processed to the church followed by choristers chanting Psalm 93 (The Lord is King). The procession then moved into the church, led by the church wardens Messrs. Hall and Rymer. The bishop started the service by reading alternate verses of Psalm 24, the clergy reading the other verses. Then followed the usual services used on these occasions, including the Rural Dean the Rector of Staunton, the Reverend R.Davies preaching the sermon. The clergy and others received Holy Communion at the hands of the Bishop. In the congregation there were two baronets, the Reverend Sir George Provost and Sir Stephen Glyn Higford Burr Esquire who had financed the chancel and whose family had given the land. Afterwards the Bishop and about one hundred and twenty guests were invited to a magnificent lunch, provided by Mrs Seys of Tutshill House (now St John's-On-The-Hill School). On the following Saturday a cottager from every dwelling in the parish was invited to a cold lunch laid out on the Vicarage lawn for about two hundred people. The school children were given two buns each and promised an afternoon of enjoyment, with tea, in a few days time.

The collections of the four services over the two days yielded £89. We are told that *"the poorer parishioners cheerfully contributed their mites to the larger gifts of their more wealthy neighbours."* The Monmouthshire Beacon concludes its report with the comment *"we cannot but congratulate the inhabitants of Tutshill upon this boon to their district- the construction of a sacred edifice of great beauty, and well adapted to worship the God of their Fathers in a becoming manner."*

In 1872 it was resolved to add a new aisle at a cost of £230 and the architect himself supervised the work to build on the addition to the church, his original design having allowed for this. The Bristol Mercury of Tuesday 18th January 1881 reported an alarming fire. *"On Sunday morning as the inhabitants of Tutshill and neighbourhood were on*

A view of the west of the church of St Luke showing the completion of the north aisle and the 20th century addition of St Luke's room.
K Underwood

their way to Divine service they were startled with the news that the pretty little church at St. Luke's was on fire. It appears that in consequence of the severity of the weather the stove had been overheated, and the woodwork around had taken fire, and when the doors of the church were opened to admit the worshippers, the air fanned the smouldering fire into a flame, and although numerous and willing hands were at once set to work, the fire was not fully mastered until damage to the extent of at least £50 had been done. We are glad to hear, however, that the place is fully insured."

In 1886 the curate, the Reverend Sales, resigned and at his leaving presentation, when it was made clear that he was a much respected curate for his work in the parish and particularly to St Luke's church, it was also noted that it was due to him that the new lamps had been installed in the church. However, a comment that his sermons were

To the Vicar of _
Tidenham _

We the undersigned while expressing our great satisfaction with the way you conduct the Services in the Parish Church, nevertheless hope that you may meet our wishes in materially shortening the morning service in any way you may think fit. _____

H F Morgan.
M. C. Morgan.   F M. Evans.
R. Beaumont-Thomas   H. M. Evans.
Rosa E. Beaumont Thomas.
Maud E. Anderson.   Alice Long
Emily C. Morgan.   Alice R. Long.
F. G. Cowburn   Henry. Belcher
C J Lindam   M. C. Belcher
Mary Lindam,   George West
                              Amelia. West.
Mary L. Lindam   Godfrey Seys.
C W Yockney
Florence Yockney   Edjar H Parker
Emily A Griffiths   A. E. Parker
Spencer J Brett
Mary Brett.
Alice Wood
William M. Rymer
Ada Rymer

An extract from a petition which is undated but asks for the vicar to shorten his services.
Gloucester Archives

sometimes a little too long may explain a surviving, but sadly undated, gentle petition from the congregation requesting that the services be shortened.

On September 7th 1888 the Rural Dean visited the parish. He was concerned that since the foundation the vicar of Tidenham had paid a curate to maintain full services at St Lukes. "*...it seemed to me, on going into this matter with the Vicar and his churchwardens that the Vicar was not legally compelled to do this and that it was the moral duty of the inhabitants of Tutshill to make St Luke's independent by maintaining their own priest*".

In 1896 with a congregation of two hundred and fifty, the church needed re-roofing since the timbers were rotten and tiles falling. A 1898 report lists the £336 costs attributed to the works and also the subscribers and donations, some of whose names are familiar as benefactors of Beachley's St John's church, St Peter and All Angels at Tidenham Chase, Stroat and Woodcroft missions as well local schools. The late Reverend Feilding Palmer, Sir W.H.Marling of Sedbury Park, H F Morgan, Miss Churchyard, Mrs Cowburn and Godfrey Seys and Mrs Price of Pen-Moel all feature prominently in the list.

The nineteenth century ended under the Reverend Charles Vincent Reydell from 1896-1900. It is recorded that, besides the new roof, there was a white silk stole worked in coloured silk made and presented by Miss Leigh, new surplices for boys, new hymn books, new hangings for the pulpit given by Miss Lindam, and collection bags made and given by Miss Callaghan.

A pre-1920 view of the chancel with central candelabra and candles in original choir stalls, steps up to the altar and the traditional Oxford Movement sanctuary. Note the wooden screen chancel rail behind the lectern on the right.
Gloucester Archives

As the Edwardian era dawned the parish records reflected a changing scene. At Easter 1904 plans were agreed to enlarge the church's vestry and the committee were to collect the subscriptions. A year later the new vestry was completed and a new heating apparatus was installed for coal and coke. Records show that, once again, the names of Mrs Fielding Palmer, Sir W Marling Bart., H F Morgan, Miss Grace, G Seys and Cowburn appear amongst many others as benefactors. In 1912 it was agreed to enlarge the churchyard by half an acre, the land being offered by SW Seys Esquire although it was not consecrated until September 1923 by the Bishop of Gloucester. There was an objection to the state of the organ, especially the keyboard, by Mr Webb and others in 1917.

The Great War showed strain on the economy and St Luke's accounts in 1918 showed a deficit due to higher fuel costs, which was paid off by Colonel Marling of Sedbury Park. Mr Parry was thanked for hauling coal and coke, free of charge. By 1919 the number of war dead from the parish was a cause for great concern and a faculty, or agreement, was sought from the Diocesan offices to erect carved oak panels at the east end of St Luke's and to record the names of the thirty fallen as a memorial. The project was paid for by Mrs Seys of Wirewoods Green who wished to give thanks for the preservation of her sons and wanted one of the wooden panels to reflect this. However, there was an objection to this. The panels were carved in 1920 by Louis de Lauver, one member of the two Belgian refugee families living in, and supported by, the parish. The dedication took place at 7pm on February 8th 1921. Later a brass plaque appeared in the porch dedicated to the Belgian refugees, and recording Mrs Sey's purchase of

St Luke's church
from the west
showing the
windows installed
in 1929.
*Gloucester
Archives*

the wooden altar surround in grateful thanks for the survival of her two sons. (See appendix 1).

On May 25th 1923 the Bishop was to be asked to consecrate new ground at Tutshill during his pastoral visit between September 1st and 3rd. During the 20s and 30s there were several discussions and calls for reports and drawings about improvements from the Diocesan architect, including the accommodation at the east end in 1922, electric lighting in 1924 and repairs to the roof in 1925. Since Mrs Stanhope had paid for the lighting in memory of her husband in 1925, it was decided that the time saved could be well utilised by the caretaker cutting the church-yard three times a year from 1926. In the same year £50 was designated for improvements.

A committee was set up in 1926 to consider whether the redecoration of the church including cleaning, preparing and painting the walls and ventilators at an estimated cost of £42 15s 0d, outweighed the need for new cassocks and surplices at £32 7s 0d. The cassocks and surplices were bought! In 1929 at the annual general meeting it was thought that reconstruction of the roof was necessary and advantageous based on the 1926 report and estimate of £270. This resulted in the new roof design with dormer windows which were removed in 1962 when the church was re-roofed.

In 1935 it was decided to buy fifty leatherette hassocks (later amended to one hundred) being sixty for St Luke's and forty for St Mary and St Peter. At the 1937 annual meeting it was reported that a chimney had come down in the last gale, the Sanctuary was damp and the church again needed re-decoration. A year later the parish magazine reported there were hopes of getting a water supply to the church as well as stating that the church was indebted to Major and Mrs Francis for a new Sanctuary carpet. The Major and his wife lived at the large house "Eastcliff" in Tutshill, worshipped at St Luke's church and had their own small access gate into the churchyard. One resident of the area recalls inadvertently sitting as a child in the pew used regularly by the Major and leaving it with great speed as he approached! The family tomb is by the church gate.

In 1960 the Quinquennial report appeared. It was noted that the nave had three pairs of dormer clerestory windows and *"a cat's cradle of dust -catching chords to allow them to be opened."* Proposed work on the church was estimated by Paterson, the Diocesan Architect to cost between £800 and £1000, with the largest item being the stripping and re-slating of the nave and north aisle, including the removal of the 1929 windows, which was finally achieved in 1962.

The Reverend Brian Green who was the incumbent from 1991-96 led the fund-raising to create a new extension including a meeting room and kitchen and toilets. The original drawings were made by Frank Granville. McCarty Associates of Chepstow prepared the final drawings, while John Hodson, builder of Coleford, constructed the extension. It was dedicated and called St Luke's Room on October 18th 1995 and during the service Brian Green was commissioned as Rural Dean by the Bishop of Gloucester. At about the same time, St Luke's church was licensed to hold weddings, having previously required special arrangements.

In 2003 the church celebrated its 150th anniversary with a series of events including a musical evening on July 4th, a Consecration Day Holy Communion on 12th August, a Flower Festival on the weekend of 12-14 September, a Birthday party on 18th October and celebratory services on 19th October.

Rotten timbers and slipping slates were once again reported as a problem and in March 2008 a major appeal was launched by the vicar the Reverend Royston Grosvenor, who was in post from 1997-2011, to raise over £100,000 for the re-roofing of the church. Later, the Parochial Church Council accepted a tender for the work from Mr Kettle. Grants totalling £18,210 were obtained from outside bodies, including £6,500 from the Gloucestershire Historic Churches Trust and £7,500 from the National Churches' Trust. The author J K

Rowling who lived as a child in Church Cottage donated a signed first edition of her book *Harry Potter and the Death Hallows* for auction. Community fund-raising events within the parish, including a Scarecrow Trail, which has now become an annual community event, produced further funds and £45,000 was raised.

At the start of 2014 discussions are taking place under the leadership of the Reverend David Traharne who was installed in October 2012, for a possible re-ordering of St Luke's which currently has the largest congregation of the three parish churches and a particularly strong youth and family element. As has been seen from the history above, the need for constant review of the use of a building does not change over the years.

THE BUILDING

The prestigious architect of St Luke's Church was Henry Woodyer Esq who had worked in William Butterfields's office but who in 1852 ran his own extensive practise from his country estate in Surrey. Woodyer, his Etonian friend Thomas Gambier Parry of Highnam and Butterfield all followed the vociferous Cambridge Camden Society, based at Cambridge University, which exercised a strong influence on church architecture for some twenty years and beyond, advocating that every part of the design of the church should be intrinsic to the solemn performance of the liturgy. They spear-headed the architectural style of Gothic Revival and in particular Decorated Gothic, with new Anglican churches having traditional chancels, altar steps and railings, open seating but no galleries.

Interestingly the Vicar, the Reverend Armstrong, was strongly influenced by the liturgical ideas of the Oxford Movement (AWN Pugin's Oxford Architectural Society) based at Oxford University which concentrated on urging a return to the traditional roots of the original catholic liturgy and the celebration of Communion every Sunday and on feast days. What emerged was an interesting combination of both these movements.

For his smaller churches Woodyer favoured either a gabled or spired bell-cote or a timber belfry and spire derived from those common in Surrey. He generally used the approved Decorated Gothic style but gave it his individual interpretation, with particularly spiky windows, tracery and oddly proportioned doorways. Other features were decorative ironwork on doors and standard-design, dated rainwater heads. St Luke's was built by Mr John Thorne of Chepstow

The distinctive Woodyer design features of spikey pointed windows and bell cote are shown in this view of St Luke's church, Tutshill.
R Clammer

The priest's seats (sedilia) with a typically Woodyer pointed design to the seat arches in the sanctuary of St Luke's church at Tutshill.
R Clammer

and originally consisted of a nave fifty-four feet long (approximately 18 metres) and twenty six feet (6.7 metres) wide, a chancel twenty six feet long and seventeen feet (5.7 metres) wide and a south porch. On the south side springing from the chancel was a turret forty-four feet high supporting a weather vane and a place to hang three small bells. In the original design there were four arcades on the north side, designed to be opened when another aisle was required. In 1872 it was resolved to add this new aisle at a cost of £230 and the architect himself supervised the work to build on the addition to the church. The roof is described in *The Buildings of Gloucestershire* as being steep with quatre-foils above the collar beams.

The roof is now identical to that originally built in 1853 but from 1929 to 1962 there were high "dormer" windows in the nave. The distinctive features of

The modern interior of St Luke's church, Tutshill with the original font made of Painswick stone lined with lead. *R Clammer*

the sanctuary area with carved stone chairs for the priests, a piscina, and the raised altar reflect the return to high church tendencies of the time.

There are several stained glass windows of note, three of which made by Wailes are original to the building of the church; one in the west end of the nave (of which only a part remains), the east window, and the third on the south side of the chancel depicting the giving of the keys to St Peter. There are two other windows of note depicting the Marriage at Cana by Heaton, Butler and Bayne and another in the west wall by Cakebread, Robey and Co. of Stoke Newington, London. They are discussed in Chapter 6 and in the tour below. Many of these are illustrated in the coloured section.

THE TOUR

Exterior

Please refer to Figure 6 for the locations used in the following tour. Standing facing the south porch of the church and moving round the building in an anti-clock wise direction, Woodyer's distinctive style is shown to the right in the first of several **rainwater heads (A)** dated 1853, seen at regular intervals high up near the roof edge.

Note the crisp outlines of the stone window moulding and the pronounced cusping of the "spiky" Decorated Gothic style **windows (B)**. Details of the content of the decorative glass windows will be included in the tour of the interior of the church below.

The distinctive **slim turret or bell-cote (C)** with three bells is the significant Woodyer feature of the outside of the church. It has its own

Fig. 6 The Church of St Luke, Tutshill

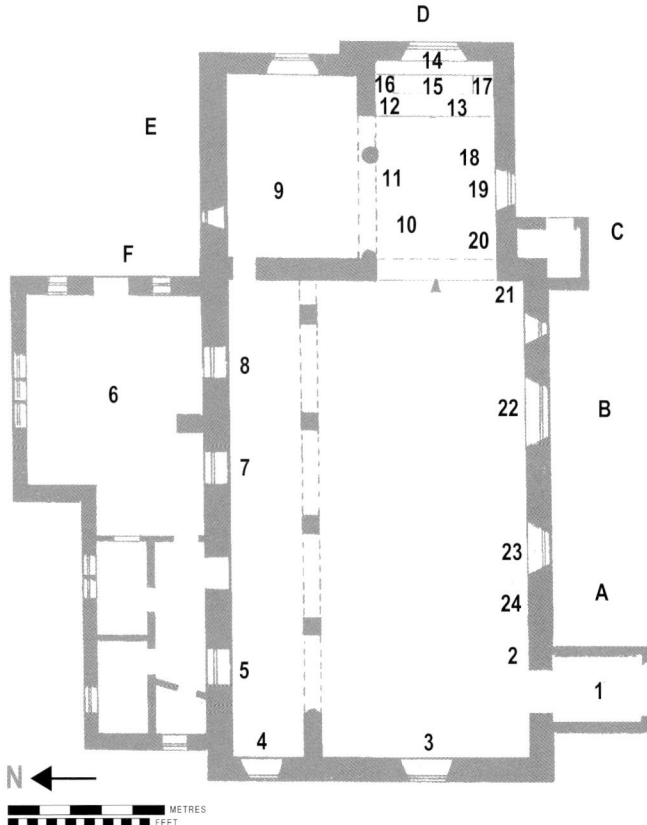

attached ringing chamber below with an access door and the whole structure is built in the same plane as the nave's east gable. On the very top is a decorative wind vane in the shape of a stylised bird.

The east window (D) will be described in more detail later and is one of the original **three** windows. **The north door (E)** into the church has a distinctive mediaeval style stone framing and decorative metalwork to the door fixings and handle.

Close by in the east wall of the extension is the **stone (F)** commemorating the opening of St Luke's room on St Luke's Day October 18th 1995. Return to the porch to begin the interior tour.

Interior

As you approach the interior of the church through the **porch (1)** note the memorial to two families of Belgian refugees supported by the parish during the First World War. One family member carved the panels on the east wall either side of the altar (see below).

Just inside the church door on the right is the **font (2)** which is original, octagonal and made of Painswick stone lined with lead. On each alternate side of the font in large raised English letters are the words Repentance, Faith, Remission, and Salvation, the alternate sides bearing emblems resembling leaves, a decorative cross and the letters IHS, being the first three letters of the name of Jesus in Greek.

In the west end of the nave there is an elegant **small window of painted glass (3)**, the first of the three made by Wailes of Newcastle and put in for the consecration of the church. This one was the gift from Captain Leyard in memory of Emily and Catherine Leyard. The report of the consecration of the church in the local paper in 1853 describes the paintings as representing Moses the law-giver, Melchisedec, an Old Testament character who was king of Salem, and John the Baptist. Only Melchisedec is seen now because the rest of the original window was removed in 1929.

On the west wall north corner of the nave is a fine **window (4)** showing Christ with young children. It was erected in October 1894 *"To the glory of God and in loving memory of Hilda, Mary, Mildred and John Lancelot Lindham"*. This window is signed by Cakebread, Robey and Co. of Stoke Newington, London.

On the north wall of the nave are three small windows, two of which are in the Arts and Crafts style. The first is **to St Matthew (5)** erected *"to the Glory of god, and in memory of James Lindham and Mary his wife"*.

Between windows lies the entrance to **St Luke's Room (6)** added in 1995-6. The foundation stone outside the east door into St Luke's Room was laid on October 18th 1995.

The middle **window** of the three, **to St Luke (7)** was erected *"to the Glory of God and in memory of Beatrice Elizabeth Jones 1904-1967"* and was made by Geoffrey Robinson in 1970.

The second Arts and Crafts **window (8) to St John** was *"erected to the Glory of God and in loving memory of Capt. Arthur Talbot RNR."*

Immediately ahead lies the **vestry (9)** and moving into **the chancel** itself note **the arcade of two arches on slim pillars (10)** which separates the vestry and organ **(11)** from the sanctuary area around the altar.

This sanctuary is a fine example of a design favoured at the time reflecting the prevailing high church movement, featuring steps up to the small altar placed against the east wall where the priest prepares the sacrament of Holy Communion with his back to the congregation. Note the false **piscina (12)**, a niche in the wall (in this case with no drain hole) used during the service of Mass or Holy Communion for storing the chalice, paten and cruets for holding the bread and wine. The functional one is behind the wall in the vestry. The decorative and colourful sanctuary **floor tiles (13)** surrounding the altar are originals by Godwin.

Above at the east end of the chancel, there is another of the three original **painted windows (14)** by Wailes of Newcastle. In the compartments are rich designs of the Baptism on the left, the Transfiguration at the top, the crucifixion in the middle and the Ascension of the Redeemer of Mankind on the right. See the coloured photo section.

Below the window, to either side of the **altar (15)** which was made by Mr M Aitken, is a **wooden reredos (16)** carved in 1920 by Louis Lauvier, a Belgian refugee and placed there by Evelyn Seys in thanksgiving for the preservation of her two sons in the Great War. The brass tablet to the left is inscribed as a memorial to the parish's dead of World War One. (See appendix 1)

To the right of the altar on the south wall is a sedilia or **double stone seat (17)** set in the wall for the clergy to use.

The **choir stalls (18)** given by Eric C Francis in 1960 and dedicated *"To the Glory of God and in memory of Mabel Edith Mary Francis 1891-1957,"* were made by Mr M Aitken at his workshop next to the old salmon fishery on The Backs at Chepstow.

Another significant stained glass **window (19)** on the south side of the chancel is the third to be put in place for the consecration of St Luke's in 1853 and represents in one compartment Our Saviour delivering the keys to St Peter, in the other the Redeemer's command to preach the Gospel. It was also painted by Mr Wailes of Newcastle.

Before re-entering the nave, note the small opening in the wall which is a **squint (20)** designed for the bell ringers in the outside bell-cote to observe the clergy in the church.

Back in the Nave, the **pulpit (21)** is original. In the south wall there are two decorated windows. The first is another later stained glass **window (22)** in three bays with Christ in the centre depicting the Resurrection. The inscription reads *"He is risen as He said"*. This window is *"in memory of Catherine, widow of John Campbell Esq. Captain R.M.L.I. died Nov 5th 1880 in her 81st year"*. This window is probably by Clayton and Bell.

The **window (23)** in the south wall of the nave nearest the church door depicts the wedding scene at Cana when Jesus calls people in from the street to join the celebrations. At the top are the words *"Surely he has borne our griefs and carried our sorrows"* and near the bottom *"Blessed are the dead which die in the Lord"*. The window was given to *"the Glory of God and in Loving memory of John, Frank, Cyril, Grace, and Ruth Armstrong"* and is a later addition, probably made by Heaton, Butler and Bayne but is described by Verey and Brooks in *The Buildings of Gloucestershire* as being *" a-typical, including no fewer than five portrait heads"*. See photograph in the coloured section. Before leaving the church note the substantial casings **(24)** on the south wall, each having a small metal hand which controlled the Tobin Tubes, a now defunct ventilation system but nevertheless considered essential by the architectural surveyor Paterson in his 1958 report for drying out the north wall!

Please note that there are full details of all the church memorials in Appendix 1.

Ordnance Survey grid reference Sheet 162 scale 1:50 000: 536945

10 STROAT EVANGELICAL CHURCH AND WOODCROFT CHRISTIAN CENTRE

HISTORY

During the second half of the 19th century several highly influential families and individuals in the parish supported the development of educational and moral activities for young and old where previously there had been few or none. The Morgan family of Tidenham House, all staunch advocates of the Temperance Society, identified Stroat and Woodcroft as two areas in particular need. During the 1880s when the Wye Valley Railway was under construction the railway workers, known as 'navvies', were housed in Woodcroft, a hamlet lying two miles outside of Chepstow on the road to Coleford and near to Tutshill, where there were several drinking houses and consequently much drunkenness. Within the south eastern outer area of the parish at Stroat there were also those poor who had no transport and needed to walk some distance to attend the church services at Tidenham.

In each case it was the prior establishment of a successful Reading or Coffee Room which led to a permanent place of worship. Georgiana Morgan, maintained the Coffee Room at Woodcroft which held services on Sundays but was also open during the week and was described by the *Chepstow Weekly Advertiser* of January 19th 1889 *"as a place of recreation in opposition to the baleful attractions which are often but too powerful in some rural districts - public houses."* After her husband's death she built Woodcroft Temperance Memorial Hall, now known as Woodcroft Christian Centre, in his memory. Stroat Mission, (or the Iron Room as it was more commonly called) now known as Stroat Evangelical Church, was also funded by the Morgan family and both were built within two years of each other, during the period 1887-9.

WOODCROFT TEMPERANCE MEMORIAL HALL
Reading and Coffee Rooms in Woodcroft

At the laying of the foundation stone of The Temperance Memorial Hall in Woodcroft on June 17th 1887, the Reverend J Hart was reported in the *Chepstow Weekly Advertiser* (of Saturday June 25th 1887) as stating that as far back as forty years previously in 1843, six years after the start of Queen Victoria's reign, it was felt that a need existed in the west of the parish for a place other than a public house where people could meet freely to enjoy social, moral and religious activities. His wife, then known as Miss Passmore, and the venerable Mrs Elderfield, who both lived in the parish in those days were moved *"by a generally expressed desire of the industrial classes"* to purchase the leasehold site on which was erected a coffee and reading room. It was not associated with the parish church or any non-conformist body although several ministers and laymen conducted services there for several years until the building closed.

The building, which had meanwhile become the Reverend Hart's property through his marriage, was then leased in 1877 to the lay-rector, Mr Thomas Henry Morgan, mainly through the encouragement of the curate the Reverend A C Gable. Services were held in the rooms by the vicar or curate and The Woodcroft Coffee and Reading Rooms (and sometimes referred to as the Tidenham Coffee Rooms) became such a success in the capable hands mostly of Miss Sofia Morgan, that it became apparent that the accommodation could not support the requirements of the neighbourhood. On the death of Thomas Henry Morgan on December 8th 1884 aged 66, Mrs Christiana Morgan and her daughters, Sofia, Emily and Fanny, took it upon themselves to provide a more suitable building.

Mrs Christiana Morgan's intention to provide such a building as a memorial to her husband was announced by her son-in-law Major Cowburn at a meeting only three months before the ceremony for the

Woodcroft
Temperance
Memorial Hall,
opened on
Tuesday 20th
December 1887.
The newer
buildings of 1966
and 2003-4 are on
the extreme right
of the picture.
R Clammer

Christiana Morgan, wife of Thomas Henry Morgan and patron of Woodcroft and Stroat centres. *Woodcroft Christian Centre*

laying of the foundation stone. In this remarkably short period, the finances were raised, and the location of the new building was chosen and the other preliminaries were completed. A newspaper article report in the *Chepstow Weekly Advertiser* of June 25th 1887 described the location as being on *"the summit of what is known as Woodcroft Common, as a situation easily accessible from the more thickly populated portion of the parish, and one of the greatest natural beauty, commanding extensive views of the Severn, the Bristol Channel, and the surrounding enchanting district."*

The laying of the foundation stone on June 17th 1887, reported under the heading *"Interesting Proceedings"*, was a significant occasion performed in the presence of a large number of parishioners with music provided by the Tidenham Brass band under the leadership of Mr E Williams. The proceedings commenced with an address by Mr Jebez Wilson, a staunch supporter of the Temperance Movement in the neighbourhood, followed by a reading from scripture, a hymn and a prayer. The first stone was laid by Mrs Morgan, whose *"announcement that it had been duly laid was received with cheers"*. The second stone was laid by Miss Sofia H Morgan, *"who, of all of the members of the family, has taken the chief interest in the management of the institution hitherto used who was presented by Mr Wilson on behalf of the members with a silver trowel ... and a wooden mallet, the trowel having the following inscription chastely engraved PRESENTED TO MISS S H MORGAN, BY THE MEMBERS OF THE TIDENHAM COFFEE ROOMS AS A TOKEN OF RESPECT ON THE OCCASION OF THE LAYING OF THE FOUNDATION STONE OF THE TEMPERANCE MEMORIAL HALL, 17TH JUNE 1887...* The third stone was laid with similar formality by Major and Mrs Cowburn and the

Thomas Henry Morgan in whose memory the Woodcroft Temperance Memorial Hall building was constructed. *Woodcroft Christian Centre*

fourth by Miss Morgan *"who superintends a similar institution in Stroat in another portion of the parish."*

Reverend J Hart described it as *"exhaustive and suitable"*. He announced that no better location could have been found in the parish. Speaking eloquently about the Morgan family who *"lived and worked amongst them in the present day"* and who had *"the best interests of the parish... very near their hearts"*, he went on to describe the drunkenness as the *"one chief blighting curse of the nation in modern times and that the inculcation of temperance principles constituted the antidote to that curse."*

The building was opened on Tuesday 20th December 1887 and attracted yet more coverage in the *Chepstow Weekly Advertiser* on Saturday December 24th 1877. Leaflets had been distributed throughout the Tidenham area stating that the building was to be open for inspection, with refreshments available. At 8 o'clock a meeting was held in the large hall which was filled to capacity and people were left standing outside. Major Cowburn opened the proceedings and Miss Sofia Morgan ably played the organ to accompany a choir of forty or fifty men and boys. Then followed a service led by the Reverend G T Turnbull during which he provided an *"able and exhaustive address upon temperance principles"* and made *"Feeling reference to the late Mr Morgan"*. The report concluded that the proceedings were *"most successful and the inhabitants of the parish of Tidenham may be heartily congratulated upon now having in their midst through the liberality of Mrs Morgan, so handsome and convenient a structure as the Morgan Memorial Temperance Mission Hall"*.

Services and weekday meetings were taken regularly by the vicar of Tidenham or one of his curates and groups were formed for young people, women and children, providing both educational and social activities. There were facilities for playing billiards and table skittles, "appliances" for chess, draughts and solitaire were provided and non-alcoholic refreshments were available. In the writing and reading room there was a selection of newspapers and popular magazines.

Christiana Morgan's daughter Fanny Sophia Cowburn laid down the strict rules regarding the trust funding and regulations for both Woodcroft Memorial Hall and the family's next venture - providing a similar facility in Stroat. Eventually a permanent member of staff was appointed to oversee the work of both Woodcroft Memorial Hall and Stroat Mission. The Western Daily Press of Friday 13 March 1931 recorded the death of the Reverend ET Wray who had been the

The refreshment room on left of the main door of Woodcroft Christian Centre with its refreshment area and original fireplace, little altered except for the addition of a modern games table.
R Clammer

superintendent of the Woodcroft Memorial Hall for twenty years. The building continued to be used regularly into the twentieth century but by the 1950s was being used less. One resident of the area attended the youth club as a child in the early 1960s. Later, as a young man, he recalled getting into the unused and unlocked building with his friends and exploring the dilapidated empty rooms. It was described by Eileen Wright in her book *"A History of Stroat Mission 1889-1989"* as quite derelict in 1973 and 1974 when the Stroat Mission congregation used the building whilst theirs was being refurbished.

Since 1975 Woodcroft Memorial Hall has been a registered charity owned by a trust of evangelical men and women from a variety of local churches and is now run as Woodcroft Christian Centre, an interdenominational facility for the local community and also providing affordable accommodation for visiting Christian groups, with a particular focus on young people. The local primary school at Tutshill uses the building for school events, parish lunches for the elderly are held on a regular basis and local youth groups meet regularly.

THE BUILDING

The original design of the building remains basically unchanged with many original features surviving. The impressive hall was constructed of local stone supplied by Messrs. Davies and Jones of Tidenham and the builder was Mr George Wilkins of Newport. Standing on an

The Temperance Memorial Hall main hall showing the magnificent American organ, built by the Mason and Hamlin Organ Co. of New York on the permanent stage.
Rose Evans

elevated position in four acres of ground, it consisted of three floors. The newspaper description describes the spacious entrance hall paved with encaustic tiles, which exists unchanged today. There was a refreshment room on the left where tea coffee, cocoa and non-alcoholic drinks were available and which was *"fitted up with all appliances for the comfort and convenience of customers"*. Today this room is used for the

The main hall just prior to redecoration at Woodcroft Christian Centre in late 2013.
R Clammer

same purpose and retains the original fire-place and other fittings, including probably the very same counter. The original bagatelle table for the *"juveniles"* has been replaced by a snooker table. The caretaker's snug accommodation was off this room and now is a kitchen.

To the right of the hall was a reading room where seats were described as *"upholstered and comfortably padded"*. Today the room has much the same feel with comfortable furniture and provision for games. The fireplaces are not visible today, but were of best Caen stone and *"the hearth stones enclosed in imitation black marble fenders are laid with tessellated pavement of a most tasteful pattern"*. There was also a small American organ supplied by Messrs Waugh & Son of Monmouth and Chepstow. Adjoining this room was a library where there were cases filled with *"instructive works"*. This room still exists, although used for another purpose.

A winding staircase joins the two main floors. *The Chepstow Advertiser* described *"passing up the staircase is the entrance to the meeting and lecture room - with an ante-room attached - a noble apartment, some 70 feet in length and 24 feet wide, which extends the whole length of the building and is capable of seating comfortably 300 persons; at one end of which is a permanent raised platform, upon which, under an alcove, is a magnificent American organ, built by the Mason and Hamlin Organ Co of New York, after a specification of the late Abbe Listz, and was supplied by Waugh & Son."* Today this meeting room, still with its stage, cannot fail to impress for its sheer size and elegance, reminiscent of a stately home. As a building for the public of the parish built by a local family who were determined to improve the facilities available it still stands as a statement to their commitment. New residential accommodation, conference and self-catering facilities were built in the grounds of the house in 1966, 2003 and 2004 to enable groups of people to stay and are a reflection of the ongoing the commitment of the current trustees.

It seems right to conclude this section on a parish building which was something extraordinary in its time, with the newspaper comment that *"the arrangements and accommodation are so perfect that they would do much credit to an establishment of far greater pretensions, and a place of larger population and much more importance than the parish of Tidenham."*

Ordnance Survey grid reference: 545956

STROAT EVANGELICAL CHURCH
HISTORY

Following the success of the Morgan's reading room for the Woodcroft area, a space was hired and set up at Wibdon Farm near Stroat by Emily Morgan in 1886 or 1887 for the initial purpose of providing a meeting place for mothers with small children on a Sunday afternoon. The success of this venture led the family to seek more permanent accommodation in the area.

In 1889, the family purchased a plot of land from the owners of Stroat House in order to provide somewhere for communion services to be held locally for people at the south eastern end of the parish, some distance away from Tidenham church. The building, which was of galvanised iron sheeting and hence always known as the Iron Room despite being officially called Stroat Mission, was opened on November 13th 1889 and was located where the former entrance to Stroat House had been. Along with the grand entrance gates, came a coachman's cottage and a coach house. Christiana Morgan left A Deed of Appointment of the Trustees of the Stroat Mission at her death which refers to the location as *"That piece or parcel of land situate at Stroat in the Parish of Tidenham in the County of Gloucester containing 1 rood and 10 perches or thereabouts with the iron Mission Room and Cottage and all other buildings erected and being erected thereon which property comprises number 1031 and part number 1030 on the Tithe map... for the said Parish"*.

Miss Emily Morgan continued to make the work at Stroat her main focus and she did much to support and encourage the members of the community. It was her original Charity for the Stroat Mission Hall that

Miss Morgan who developed Stroat Mission or "Iron Room" with her sister.
Stroat Evangelical Church

had to *"be applied in keeping in repair the Stroat Mission Hall and cottage and in carrying on the services and Mission work as long as the Trustees shall think the annual income sufficient"*. She did this in addition to supporting her sister Sophia with Woodcroft and both establishments remained a joint project for over 80 years.

Sunday services were held at Stroat Mission by the Vicar of Tidenham Parish church or one of his curates, this time during the

Stroat Mission, or
the "Iron Room", in
the mid-20th
century
Stroat Evangelical
Church

afternoon from 3.30-4.30, to avoid clashing with the services at
Tidenham. Current worshippers describe how Sankey hymn books
were used, some of which remain to this day, having survived several
floods and a fire! It soon became the regular meeting place not only of
the original mothers with young children group on Sunday afternoons
but also mid-week evening meetings for boys under 18. The older ones
played snooker, bagatelle, draughts and chess. The younger boys played
Snap and Happy Families. Girls attended meetings in the winter and
did needlework and knitting. Soup was served to the poor and needy
during the week. Interestingly, local records state that the women and
girls were given an outing in the summer, whereas the working men
and boys were given a special roast beef Christmas dinner followed by
Christmas pudding all washed down with vast amounts of non-
alcoholic beverages!

The Stroat Inn, located opposite Stroat House, was popular with
the local men, who made offensive remarks to the passing girls. The
Mission benefactor, Christiana Morgan, therefore bought the pub and
then promptly closed it down!

Following Emily's death in 1914, the work was carried on by Miss
Eunice Challis, followed by her cousin Mrs Esther Challis and Miss
Milray. These were all ladies who worshipped at Tidenham parish
church, as well as overseeing the work at Stroat. Missionary sales of

Mrs Eileen Wright, the pastor's wife, cooking in the open after the devastating fire which ran through Stroat Mission in January 1976. Stroat Evangelical Church

work were regularly held to raise money for the China Inland Mission, the Churchmen's Missionary Society and the Mission to Lepers. These sales became popular in the district and served a social purpose as well as raising large sums of money.

Among the regulations drawn up by Emily's sister Fanny Cowburn, had been the fact that the management of the Stroat Mission should come under the hands of the trustees of the Memorial Temperance Hall at Woodcroft, and that it be continued as an Evangelical Protestant Mission following her own death. Thus it was that in February 1931, the charity continued in the hands of the joint trustees of both establishments through a document dated 28th April 1932 which saw the building vested in the trustees of Tidenham (Woodcroft) Memorial Hall.

The *Gloucester Journal* of March 13 1948 recorded the death of Mr Gilbert Underwood Roberts who had retired from the Caravan Mission to village children in 1946 due to failing health and then accepted the oversight of Stroat Mission and Woodcroft Memorial Hall. In 1950, the Reverend W Hill and his wife were appointed to lead the work at Stroat and Woodcroft. The manse attached to the mission was very small and their daughter Daphne had to sleep in what was described as a 'hut' at the back of the hall. It is said that Gladys Aylward, the missionary in China who led one hundred orphaned children across the mountains to Siberia to flee the invading Japanese in 1940, also shared this hut on one occasion when visiting Stroat during her ten year period in Britain before returning to Taiwan for the rest of her life.

After seven years the Reverend Hill moved on and in 1957 the Reverend Leslie Musgrove was appointed. Just as he was settling in disaster struck and there was a serious setback. One night there was a torrential downpour and the water levels, which were never far below the ground, rose rapidly with the waters soon reaching window sill height, badly flooding the building.

THE SEVERN VALLEY MISSIONS

STROAT MISSION & WOODCROFT HALL.

Young men and maidens, old men and children: praise the Lord. (Ps 145.12-13)

The bus from Stroat Mission toured the rural communities bringing in children and adults for services, pioneered by the Reverend Alan Wright.
Stroat Evangelical Church

After some years Mr Ken Cracknell of Beeches Farm at Tidenham Chase, shouldered the responsibility of the post as pastor, then in 1963 the Reverend Alan Wright was appointed and was to go on to serve for twenty years. Catastrophe struck again when on a very windy day the blowlamp of a roofing specialist working on an extension to the building caused the roof of the Manse to catch fire, causing serious damage. However, it may have proved to be a blessing in disguise for as part of the roof repairs, two upstairs bedrooms were added to the building.

During this time the Mission's two mini-buses became a familiar sight in the rural lanes collecting children from Sedbury, Tutshill and Woolaston and Alvington, each making two journeys before Sunday school, Bible Club and often other events in between.

In 1972 the Reverend and Mrs William Hill were appointed managers and in the same year a friend of the Mission offered to help in providing a new church. During the years of the refurbishment the church met at the Woodcroft Memorial Hall, until 1975 when the new building was finally finished.

Thereafter known as Stroat Mission Non-Denominational Evangelical Church, the decision was made that it should be operated

A group of young worshippers celebrating Christmas at Stroat Mission before the major refurbishment, showing the dark wooden wall and ceiling panelling and the organ to the left.
Stroat Evangelical Church

independently from its Woodcroft partner. This was through a deed of trust dated 31st March 1976 for it to be set up as a church unconnected with Woodcroft Memorial Hall. The church reached its peak when the fleet of buses going around the rural lanes bringing children in for the Sunday School delivered so many that adults were forced to meet in a room in a neighbouring farm to have their own church services.

After a while the Reverend Colin Tamplin joined the church,

The light and airy meeting room and refreshment area of Stroat Evangelical Church in December 2013 – in contrast to the original dark wooden panelled interior shown above.
R Clammer

The outside of Stroat Evangelical Church showing the church building on the left and what originally was the coachman's cottage to the right, now the manse.
R Clammer

serving for five years, and the name changed once more to Stroat Evangelical Church, its current name. Leadership passed to the Elder, Mr Ron Edmond Senior, then to Mr Nick Baldwin and to the present pastor Chris Rees who was inducted in 2004. On November 14th 2009 at 6.30 pm a special one hundred and twenty years anniversary event was held at the church. Besides the regular services, there is still a meeting time for mothers/carers with young children and the young in the area still have a session to themselves, echoing the original ethos of the Morgan family when they established the Mission in 1889.

THE BUILDING

The original site had several buildings including the coach house and the coachman's cottage which belonged to Stroat House. Entering the gates to the current church, there is a detached building on the left which replaced the old coach house and is now used for children's activities. The building on the right, the manse where the pastor lives, was the coachman's two-roomed cottage. The main building which can be seen straight ahead with its floor to ceiling windows and glazed entrance door is a far cry from the original 'Iron Room' which was exactly that - a basic wood framed building with galvanised iron walls and roof. Inside there was originally dark wood panelling from floor to ceiling and heavy curtains divided the interior into three separate areas. One 1960s picture of the interior indicates a substantial organ to the left and in another there is a raised dais and a piano to the right. The dark cladding is evident in both. In the mid sixties the exterior was given a face-lift with a coat of blue paint on the walls and a grey roof.

The whole building was improved significantly in November 1975 with an extension, new cladding and roof, which is how it is today. There appeared to have been problems getting the terms of the re-building sorted and initial plans to completely re-build on the site were thwarted. However, eventually a substantial amount of the work was carried out by friends and members of the church. The Iron Room was replaced by a new, custom-built church and the manse was modernised.

In stark contrast to the dark cladding of the mid-twentieth century, the current building is bright and airy with plain walls. An entrance lobby leads into a spacious room which forms the worship area of the church. There is a small dais at the east end above which are written the words *Jesus Christ is Lord*. There are pine roof trusses and beams open to view and the north wall has large ceiling to floor windows. This room has a flexible seating arrangement which means it can be used for a variety of purposes. On the south wall more windows looking onto a meeting room, and a large, well equipped kitchen area.

Ordnance Survey Grid reference Sheet 162 scale 1:50 000: 573975

11 ST MICHAEL AND ALL ANGELS CHURCH, TIDENHAM CHASE

HISTORY

Tidenham Chase lies on the Chepstow to Coleford road in an elevated area which, to this day, is still extremely rural in nature. During the 1840s, with the parish church at Tidenham some two miles away, a need was felt amongst the well-to-do of the parish to offer more, particularly for the poor and those living on the extremity of the parish. The 1815 Inclosure Award had taken in waste land on Tidenham Chase of which about one hundred and five acres, called informally 'Parson's Allotment', had become glebe land by 1843 which meant that it was included in the property owned by the church and was to be owned and managed by the local vicar. Reverend Armstrong, at his own expense, quickly set about extending one of the properties on this land, Glebe Cottage, to create a school room which could also be used to offer an additional Sunday service particularly for the benefit of the neglected rural community living on Tidenham Chase. On 12 September 1850 the school was completed and licensed for services.

Mead quotes an extract from Carter describing it as:

"…a picturesque sight, our little school room on a fine Sunday afternoon. It stood on a fine commanding situation with an extensive view, the home scenery wild enough for anything. The simple Latin cross on the gable alone distinguished it from any wholly secular building; and under its shelter used to be gathered together a goodly flock of some of England's least polished sons, filling the room to overflowing…. only disturbed in their devotions by the noise of the geese of the old woman who lived in the adjoining cottage, and which used, sadly to their mistress's disquiet, to dispute with us the occupation of the ground."

As the population in the area increased further, the need was identified for a permanent local place of worship closer than the parish church at Tidenham and the chapel-of-ease at Tutshill, which had been built in 1853. There was substantial support from the Bishops of the diocese, local clergy and wealthier benefactors in the area and on April 5th 1888 the chapel of St Michael and All Angels was consecrated by the Bishop of Gloucester and Bristol. *The Chepstow Weekly Advertiser*

St Michael and All Angel's church at Tidenham Chase being built.
Audrey Vaughan

of April 7th 1888 described the event as starting

"...at about half past eleven o'clock, after the arrival of the Bishop and attendant clergy, and they having been robed at a cottage adjacent to the new building, they were met at the gate by the Tidenham surpliced choir, who preceded the Bishop, who, with the attendant clergy, at the entrance to the church was received by the Registrar C. Bonner Esq., the Deputy Chancellor, Canon Mayne, and the churchwardens of the parish, Messrs T. Evans and J. P. Rymer... The procession then entered the church...the Bishop then being seated at the communion table the deed of conveyance of the site and building was presented to him and laid upon the table and by him ordered to be registered. The sentence of the consecration was then read by the deputy Chancellor, and signed by the Bishop and by him ordered to be registered and laid upon the table. The service of the day was then read by the Reverend C Townshend."

Miss Mary Ann Churchyard who lived at Chase House and donated the stone for the church of St Michael and also continued to support the church in many ways.
Alan White

The Bishop in his address praised the work of the Reverend Feilding Palmer who had not only taken services for nearly twenty-one years in the schoolroom close by, but had funded the church to a considerable amount. He also referred to *"their dear sister Miss Churchyard for her generosity in presenting the site for the church."* After the service *"a RECHERCHE luncheon, provided by Mr T P Harrison, of the George Hotel, Chepstow, which gave the utmost satisfaction, was partaken of in the school room a short distance from the site of the church, to which about 60 sat down."*

The Reverend Feilding Palmer was one of the foremost of several benefactors. He funded the building of the church at a cost of £1030, equipped it internally, paid for a curate to deliver the services and later helped to fund on-going repairs and renewals. He first officiated in Tidenham during 1864 but over the following twenty or thirty years performed considerable service to this relatively deprived area, thus carrying on the work of the Rev. Armstrong, who had left the parish in 1853. He was clearly a generous benefactor who also visited the sick and poor and, when he could no longer do so, contributed £500 to a fund to provide an additional curate. Thus the curacy was endowed but not to the full amount, with the vicar of Tidenham expected to make

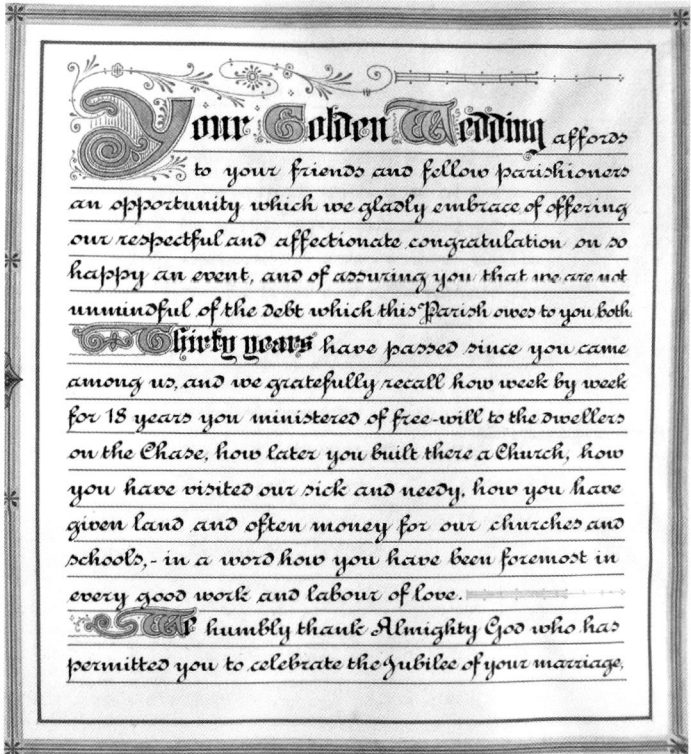

A page from the 50th wedding anniversary commemorative book given by the parishioners to Reverend Fielding Palmer and his wife on 14th October 1896 describing their gratitude for his generosity in time and money spent for the benefit of the parish, in particular at Tidenham Chase. *Gloucester Archives*

up the deficiency. Feilding also bought pews for seating one hundred at a cost of £1200 and his wife gifted three panels of stained glass in a colourful mosaic reredos located behind the altar and made by Messrs Powell of Whitefriars. (See tour below). When he died in 1897, his wife dedicated two memorial windows to him in the church. A beautiful commemorative book created by the parish to celebrate the Fielding Palmers' golden wedding anniversary extols his virtues as a priest and benefactor.

There were several other significant benefactors within the Chase area. Miss Mary Ann Churchyard, who lived at what was then the Chase Farm House, gave the land on which the church was built and paid for the expense of quarrying the stone. She allegedly actually pegged out the land prior to the starting of the building. Following the death of both her parents in 1840, she had come to live with her uncle Henry Churchyard and after his death, continued to live at Chase Farm until her own death in 1899. During the curacy of Charles Vincent Reynall from 1896-1900 it is recorded that Miss Mary Ann Churchyard gave St Michaels new surplices and psalters, red silk pulpit and matching alms bags which were worked by Miss Jotsam. She died on 11th of October 1899 aged 79 and the Bath Chronicle and Weekly Gazette of Thursday 14th December 1899 describes how amongst other bequests, she *"devised her freehold property at Tidenham and all her other real estate to her cousin Fanny Grace, absolutely."*

Miss Fanny Grace, Miss Churchyard's much younger cousin, came to visit from London and liked the area so much that she stayed on, living with Miss Churchyard. In 1894 the ladies renamed the farm house Chase House when a new Chase Farm house was built by the Sedbury Park Estate. She was probably the most significant benefactor into the early twentieth century, coming from a London family and being of independent means, even before her inheritance from her cousin. At one point she is described as having six domiciliary workers and thirteen agricultural workers. She became the church organist and went on to serve in that post for thirty five years, living in Chase House after Miss Churchyard's death. She continued to support the church including purchasing new gates, donating redecoration costs and she bequeathed substantial funding to charity for the benefit of the church. In 1932, at the age of eighty, she moved out of Chase House to Stroat House to live as a companion to the Joyce family prior until her death at the age of eighty-five on January 14th 1937.

Other significant benefactors of the church and Chase School were relatives of Fanny Grace living in Clifton, Bristol – her aunt Miss Henrietta Grace (1818-1891) and her Merchant Venturer husband Charles Bowles Hare who was one time High Sheriff of Bristol. Henrietta donated the altar for the church and they were both frequent visitors to the school, the church and Chase House.

Following the building of the church in 1889 the Rural Dean visited St Michaels and All Angels and found it in excellent order. Estimates for the 1901 refurbishment of the parish church included quotes for distemper at St Michaels. On Michaelmas Day 1905 the bishop consecrated the churchyard, dedicated a memorial window to Miss Churchyard and gave a good address about the administration of angels.

After the end of the First World War, roof repairs took place and trees were cut down in the churchyard and sold. The money for the timber was spent on re-painting, the Bishop having stated that the balance from the sale of the trees was to be used for repairs to benefit the property. In 1919 a deficit was recorded and repairs were made to the bell frame. Lamps from Tutshill church were donated and transferred to the Chase church in 1925.

In 1932 the annual church meeting reported that Chase Sunday school had begun and also noted that the redecoration of the church

The interior of Chase church from the Fielding-Palmer anniversary commemorative book circa 1896. Note the decorated altar by Powells and the reredos behind the altar. *Gloucester Archives*

St Michael and All Angels church in 1928 with probably the wife & daughter of the photographer Mr R Workman by the church gates.
Mary Bruton

had been paid for entirely by Miss Grace. Two years later she presented the church with a pair of new gates in memory of her friend Mrs Hare. Once again, at a point when the building was nearing fifty years old, Fanny Grace came to the aid of the church. In her will of 1937 she raised an additional £4,000 endowment for the church to increase that given by Reverend Feilding Palmer and also gave £1000 to the vicar and churchwardens of Tidenham for the repair of the fabric, the salary of an organist and the maintenance of the church. In the same year, it was reported that the roof needed attention so no doubt this money

The Tidenham Chase choir circa 1928. Middle row far left Anthony Savery, middle row centre Idris Stone.
Mary Bruton

St Michaels and All Angels at Tidenham Chase. *R Clammer*

would have been very welcome. She also donated a cottage to be leased to members of the Church of England, who were not permitted to keep a dog or poultry but were to be given one ton of best coal each year. On 14 April 1938 a request for a memorial bronze tablet to Fanny Grace at a cost of £35 was granted.

New metal gates were installed in 2012, replacing the badly rotted wooden memorial gates to Mrs Hare. Despite its splendidly isolated position on Tidenham Chase the church of St Michael and All Angels continues to be used regularly by a loyal congregation for Sunday Evensong services and Communion.

A detail of the altar and reredos at St Michael and All Angels church in 2014 showing the detailed mosaic glass work by Powells & Son, a company which produced similar mosaics in the roof of St Paul's cathedral. *R Clammer*

THE BUILDING

Comprising of nave and chancel in the Early English Gothic style, St Michael and All Angels was built by Mr J Haines of Cowbridge Road, Cardiff during the period 1888-9 and designed by Sidney Gambier-Parry (1859-1940). He was the son of Thomas Gambier Parry (1816-88), artist, art collector and philanthropist who lived at Highnam Court near Gloucester. The latter inherited a fortune from the East India Company and combined strong religious faith with musical and artistic talents. He built and endowed a school, parsonage and church at Highnam. Sidney had a practise in Highnam Court and in London and was articled for Sir Arthur Blomfield. His buildings were clearly inspired by the architect Henry Woodyer, an Etonian school friend who designed St Luke's church. Parry also built Bentham Church at Badgeworth, and restored of the church of St Michael at Bulley, near Churchham. In 1930 he retired into a tall, unpretentious rectory in Duntisbourne Rouse in Gloucestershire where he repaired the church.

The plan of the original building consisted of a nave 40 feet long by 22 feet wide (13 metres) with a 4 feet 6 inches (1.5 metres) wide aisle flanked by open pews capable of seating ninety eight people. There is a south porch, vestry and chancel, and a stone bell turret surmounting the west gable containing one bell. The original building had a small amount of colouring in the plaster, making a pleasant contrast with the Farleigh Stone. The chancel had seating for another ten choir members, plus two prayer desks. The windows throughout were made of cathedral tinted glass, in diamond shaped and square panes with a ruby border. The church was decorated with some good quality stained glass and mosaics by Powells, the very well respected company whose work is in St Paul's cathedral, and stained glass by Heaton, Butler and Payne, including the east window given by Mr and Mrs Duckworth. Both have been described in chapter 6 and are illustrated in the colour section. The striking oak altar given by Mrs Hare, Fanny Grace's aunt, (see tour below) and the reredos behind the altar, the gift of Mrs Feilding Palmer, reflected the extent to which the benefactors were prepared to pay for taste and quality of the time in what was essentially a modest rural church.

THE TOUR

Please refer to figure 7 for the tour. As you approach the church you go through the modern **churchyard gates (1)** which were made in 2012

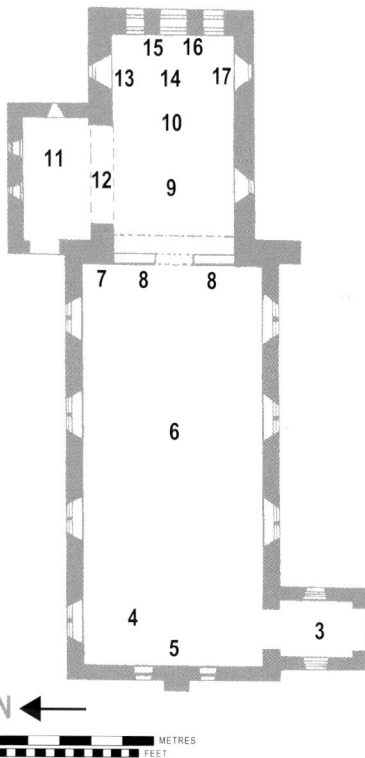

N ←

METRES
FEET

replacing the previous memorial wooden gates made by Eric Francis in 1935 and donated by Fanny Grace. Note the **steep bellcote** for a single bell at the **west end (2)** and the fact that the church is built of local stone.

Entering the church via **the porch (3)** you see the nearby **font (4)** at the west end of the nave made of Farleigh Down Stone with a Tidenham Chase stone shaft.

The **west window (5)** made in 1906 is attributed to Powells and consists of two lancet windows with a quatre-foil light above them.

The nave (6) has narrow lancet windows arranged in couples in the north and south walls. Look up and note that the roof is of pitch pine and open timber framed. Note also the unaltered rendered interior which originally would have had some colour.

Approaching the chancel, note the oak **pulpit (7)** on the left built by Messrs Jones and Willis who also built the altar.

Entering the chancel, the **chancel screen (8)** is one of Parry's furnishings consisting of a low stone screen with light wrought iron cresting executed from the architect's designs by Messrs Gardner of Bristol.

The **chancel (9)** is 22 feet (7 metres), has stained and varnished pitch pine seating and a roof which is barrel vaulted in pitch pine and divided into panels with moulded ribs. Note the chancel aisle and floor is paved with ornamental "encaustic" **tiles (10)**.

The vestry (11) is entered under an archway on the left, screened off from the chancel with stained pitched pine and a draining piscina. There is an **organ (12)** on the north side of the chancel. On the north side of the altar area is a small lancet window below which is a **stone credence or shelf (13)**, used during Communion services.

The original **altar (14)** is made of oak divided into three panels, deeply recessed and coloured, with the centre panel containing a fluted cross of letters and what was described at the time as *"the conventional* *scrolls of vines and wheat".* It was designed by Parry, coloured by Heaton and Butler and made by Messrs Jones and Willis who also constructed the pulpit.

Behind the altar are three highly decorative small **reredos panels (15)** filled with bright mosaics made by James Powell and Sons whose importance has been described in chapter 6. They were gifted by Mrs Henry Feilding, the wife of the church's main benefactor. The figure of the Lamb fills the centre panels with the side panels containing figures of angels in the act of adoration.

The 1889 east **stained glass window (16)** was designed by Gambier Parry and made by Heaton, Butler and Payne. It depicts an upper central picture of Christ in the Act of Benediction with the patron saint of the church St Michael in the lower section. The side lights show adoring angels. There is a memorial to Miss Phillips of Pen Moel House and two windows as a memorial to Feilding Palmer who was the original major benefactor of the church and died in 1897. The window was provided by his widow.

To the right of the altar are the **sedilia (17)**, the stone priests' seats.

Before leaving the church note the **two brass memorials** to Mary Ann Churchyard and Fanny Grace both women who, as discussed in the history section above, were highly significant in the life of the church.

Ordnance Survey Grid reference Sheet 162 scale 1:50 000: 556988

12 THE CHAPEL OF ST GEORGE, BEACHLEY BARRACKS

HISTORY

The sudden clearance of Beachley village for a camp of huts to house six thousand Royal Engineers and a host of German prisoners-of-war, brought in to build Chepstow Shipyard No 2, has been outlined in Chapter 7. After the closure of the shipyards, the site remained a disused eyesore until the War Office founded the Boys' Technical School which arrived and took over the buildings in 1924. In 1929 the name was changed to the Army Technical School (Boys) and from the outset it was envisaged that the new school should be imbued with a public school ethos, giving boys, often from less privileged backgrounds, the chance to receive a good balanced education for life whilst undergoing trade and military training.

The first chapel in 1924 was located in a hut which had formerly been a canteen building. In that same year the Chaplain-General for the army, the Right Reverend Bishop Taylor Smith confirmed ninety-two candidates in October. Through the efforts of the first chaplain, the Reverend E C Douglas, and his successors the chapel began to take shape and acquire the trappings of a proper place of Anglican worship. In its early days, the well-meaning padres hung prints of spiritual subjects by Italian and other Masters with the intention of giving the boys inspiration.

The year 1926 was an active one for the chapel. The padre, mindful that it was a temporary building, complained that the King's Regulations and Army funds made no provision for garrison churches with the result that £50 was advanced, and the money was swiftly swallowed up in repairs to the chapel building. Most of the fittings, including the altar and the pulpit,were made by staff and boys in the workshops as part of their trade training. A tradition was thus initiated out of necessity that saw the production of many fine pieces of work in wood, stone and metal, with the paint shop making contributions including a board bearing the names of the School padres. The padre felt that this was admirable and reflected mediaeval guild practice.

The Chapel's ministry co-existed with that of the parish of Tidenham and the Vicar, the Reverend R P Steer, was a frequent visitor. The padre, staff and boys attended services at St Luke's, St Mary and St Peter and the nearby St John's churches. The Bishops of Gloucester and Tewkesbury between them visited the school for confirmation services twice a year, often with the Vicar assisting. Numbers of candidates were often high, as many as one hundred and thirty boys at a time.

In 1927 the Guild of St George was founded for soldiers, an off-shoot of the Church of England's Men's Society. In the same year the chapel was described as being *"very pretty"* after staff wives had decorated it. Apart from the Sunday church parades that were compulsory, there were many other services during the year: confirmations, regimental celebrations, a Christmas *Nine Lessons and Carols* service, Harvest Festival and Armistice Sunday. The chapel was developing into a very active spiritual centre for the school. A feature that seems very novel for the time was the holding of Workshop Services in the Carpenters' Shop. At harvest festival, later in the school's life, artefacts from the workshops went on display in the chapel along with the usual vegetables, corn sheaves and fruit.

At the outbreak of the Second World War the padre was the Reverend Selwyn Cox. One hundred and fifty nine boys and three members of staff were confirmed in the April with the Vicar of Tidenham, the Reverend G R Newman, and the Vicar of Woolaston, the Reverend Braithwaite, assisting the Bishop of Gloucester. There were Lenten services, and frequent programmes of religious films in the camp cinema. The building itself continued to be refurbished and embellished by the work of boys in the workshops, and gothic windows were inserted in the east end. In November 1939 the Armistice Service was poignantly renamed "A Service of Remembrance and Re-dedication", as many of the boys were due to join the conflict. It is perhaps significant that a further one hundred and eleven boys were confirmed in the chapel by the Lord Bishop of Tewksbury that same month. In his message to them he included an exhortation from the Book of Revelation, *"Be thou faithful unto death and I will give thee a crown of life"*. In view of the many names in the Book of Remembrance, which were still being collected in the aftermath of the war in 1947, it is sobering to think that many of those confirmed in 1939 did, in fact, achieve that crown.

By September 1940 the effects of the war were being felt at the camp. Four hundred soldiers from the evacuation at Dunkirk arrived to unwind, debrief and be given medical and other care. A voluntary service for them at the chapel was well attended and it was reported that, judging by their magnificent giving of alms, they must have appreciated that opportunity of giving thanks to almighty God for their safe return. Early in the year epidemics had reduced the number of communicants and the black-outs made evening activities difficult, especially for the Guild of St George. On November 9th a Junkers 88 aircraft dropped two bombs on the workshops and strafed the camp, killing Apprentice Tradesman Thornton (aged sixteen) and wounding a sergeant. The padre was very much in demand at this time and the chapel was seen as a sanctuary. Thornton was buried in the nearby military cemetery next to St John's Chapel at Beachley.

In 1942 a new padre arrived, the Reverend Maxwell E Cooper, who tried to maintain a normal routine of chapel life. In the remaining years of the war, activities were often interwoven with those of Tidenham and Chepstow, and baptisms and marriages took place in both St George's chapel and at St John the Evangelist church. Despite the recent air raid, a garden party was held in the Army Technical School playing fields and, as the threat of German air superiority waned, gymkhanas and open days became a popular local summer feature. Central to these occasions was the Drum-Head Service, taken by the Padre who stated in *The Robot*, the journal of the Technical School, that there were more people at the service than the previous year (1941), which boded well for the takings later on. While the service was in progress, he wondered why it was that *"we used to be able to lift the roof off the school chapel with these well known hymns, yet out in the open we sounded more like the sigh of the wind in the trees. It was just the same last year. We improved a little when the microphone was moved nearer the choir, and so had a lead to follow, but even then it was not too brilliant. If we could have all put our heart and soul into it, like the treble in the choir singing "stand up, stand up for Jesus" what a volume of sound there would have been. That's the way to sing, right from the lungs. I should have signed him on for the next concert. His singing voice, and the speaking voice of the Chaplain who read the second lesson, were my deepest impressions of the service."*

In 1943 the chapel choir repeated a successful carol service in Tidenham parish church and the congregation was impressed. The padre noted *"But I like best the remark of the old lady after the service, 'well, I am sure the Lord must be very pleased with the boys for telling us the old, old, story of his birthday so nicely.' "*

As the war drew to a close, the chapel of St George continued its

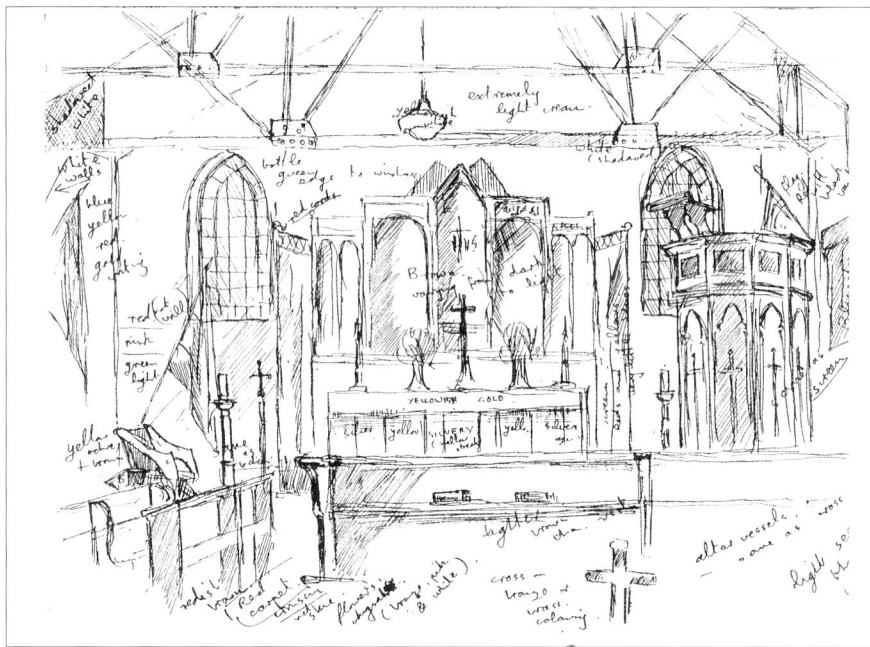

A sketch for a gouache painting made in 1951 or 1952 of the interior of the first Chapel of St George..
K Underwood

active life in the school and the local community. There was a staff wedding in St John's church, the first of its kind where both parties were involved with the Army. The Vicar returned from his duties with the Royal Army Chaplains' department to continue to preach in the chapel and assisted at the 1946 confirmation service which was conducted by the Bishop of Gloucester, Dr Woodward. The Guild of St George was revived and prospered in the new climate of hope.

In 1958 the boys of 55B Group donated a bell from the troop ship *Cameronia* as a passing out gift. In the same year there were seven baptisms, one marriage and seventy one confirmations (including eight girls and three boys from staff families). The next year saw a complete redecoration and partial refitting of the chapel, including a new altar and choir stalls made in the workshops. While work was in progress Holy Communion services took place in St. John's church. Once completed the chapel also became the home for the members of the free-church congregation. The active Sunday school that had met in the Army Garrison School, at nearby Pennsylvania, also moved to the chapel.

Plans were now afoot to rebuild the Army Technical School and St

PROGRAMME

ARMY APPRENTICES SCHOOL

Drumhead Service and Gymkhana

2nd JULY, 1950.

2.30 p.m. - Drumhead Service.
(The Collection is for the Memorial Library, Chepstow).

3.10 „ - Band will beat Retreat.

3.40 „ - Gymkhana opens.

4 „ - Physical Training Display.

6.15 „ - Draw for Raffle.

6.45-7.5 - 2nd Physical Training Display.

8.30 „ - Side Shows close.

8.30-9 - Band Programme.

8.45 „ - Draw for Lucky Ticket.
(See below).

9 „ - God Save the King.

NOTE.— Every 3d. spent at any stall entitles the spender to a ticket in the Draw :—

First Prize	...	...	£2 0 0.
Second Prize	...	...	£1 10 0.
Third Prize	...	...	£1 0 0.

Davies & Roberts Ltd., Printers, Chepstow.

A 1950 advertising bill for the Army Apprentice's School Drumhead Service and Gymkhana to raise funds for Chepstow Memorial Library. *Tidenham History Group*

George's chapel was not to be forgotten. In 1960 the padre, the Reverend Scammell commented in his *Robot* notes:

"The new camp is rising phoenix like from the ashes of the old. Even the church will eventually be replaced by a new building more in keeping with its surroundings. There are some who regret this, and feel that the old church so skillfully converted from an ordinary hut, worshipped in and cared for and steadily improved over nearly forty years, enshrines so much tradition and spirit that it would be wrong to replace it. But it is a not structurally sound enough to last indefinitely, and its appearance would no longer seem worthy if it was the only surviving black and white breeze block hut in the camp, especially when the Roman Catholic and free church congregations also have proper church buildings of their own."

In the following year Padre Scammell's successor, the Reverend AD Bartlett, noted in his "Padre's Corner" the first ever visit of an Archbishop to the school chapel on 28th June 1961 when the Arch Bishop of Wales, the Most Reverend A E Morris came to preach. He also described how, when the school was rebuilt, there would be a new chapel. The architect's design had been approved by the Chaplain-General and building was scheduled to begin in 1962. The new chapel would be considerably bigger than the present one and more contemporary in design. He went on to say that the architect had made provision for incorporating into the new chapel many of the furnishings of the existing chapel, including the memorial Chapel and the Ford memorial window, the stained glass windows and the pipe organ.

During its last years the old St George's chapel continued to attract the attention of a variety of visiting clergy, including the Bishop to the Forces, the Bishop of Maidstone, the Bishop of St Asalph and the chaplain of Monmouth School. In *The Robot* of June 1962 the padre, Reverend H W Hutchings wrote *"We look forward to the day when we shall see a permanent building dedicated and consecrated and capable of seating a thousand souls, in which the School may be able to worship as one corporate body and not, as perforce at present, in two separate parades."*

THE NEW CHAPEL

The dream was realised on May 22nd 1963 when, on a site close to the old chapel, the foundation stone was laid for the new Chapel of St George by Mrs Ford, the widow of the school's first commandant, Lt. Colonel (later Brigadier) V T R Ford. The afternoon service was conducted by the school Chaplain, the Reverend A D Bartlett, and was attended by boys of all Companies, members of the permanent staff, their families and invited guests. The foundation stone was dedicated by the Assistant Chaplain-General Western Command, the Reverend A Hodgins. The Commandant, Colonel P N Keymer of the Yorkshire and Lancashire Regiment, read the lesson. An octet from the school

The new Chapel of St George at Beachley Barracks being built in 1963 with roof trusses in position. The chapel was consecrated in May 1964.
K Underwood

military band accompanied the singing. After the ceremony a bouquet and the silver trowel used for the stone laying were presented to Mrs Ford.

At the end of the year a new padre, the Reverend J A Westmucket, who was particularly keen to research the history of the first chapel, began preparing for the completion and dedication of the new building. Services during the year included Harvest Thanksgiving Service from which gifts were made to the St Lawrence Hospital in Chepstow, and Remembrance Sunday.

The dedication of the new St George's Chapel took place with due ceremony on May 31st 1964. It was conducted by the Venerable Archdeacon I D Neill, Chaplain to the Queen and Chaplain-General. The order of service began with the Chaplain-General, attended by the chaplains and wardens, being escorted to the sanctuary entrance, where the Commandant said: *"Venerable Sir, on behalf of all ranks of the Army Apprentices' School, Chepstow, I ask you to dedicate this chapel to the glory of God, in honour of St George, and to the service of this school."* The school collect was also said, reminding those in the congregation of the supreme sacrifice made by over two hundred and fifty former apprentices during the Second World War.

In 1964 the Bishop of Maidstone confirmed two hundred and three apprentices and five sons and daughters of members of the staff. In the same year the Beachley Old Boys' Association paid £106 18s 3d from its funds for a new chapel bell. The old bell became an alarm bell outside the new guardroom. In 1965 the school became the Army Apprentices' College and in 1969 the new padre the Reverend D Spillman, is remembered for his use of humour in his approach to aspects of his work which put him more on the same wave length as that of the boys. His arrival coincided with the making of substantial pews for the nave of St George's as well as the consecration of St Joseph's the Roman Catholic chapel (see chapter 11) and the opening of St David's, the Free-Church chapel (see chapter 12), thus giving the College a very sound spiritual foundation. In the next year he was joined by a second padre, the Reverend A J Spivey serving St David's Free Church.

On 7th November 1971 the new padre, the Reverend R B Morris presided over the installation of a splendid new organ which was dedicated by the Bishop of Gloucester, the Right Reverend Basil Guy. In the spring of the next year the collections at chapel services in less than four months enabled donations to fifteen charities amounting to £445.

Lowering the memorial stone in 1973 outside St George's chapel at the Army Apprentices' College.
Robot magazine

The College celebrated its Golden Jubilee in 1973 and Princess Ann came to celebrate. In St George's the memorial chapel had been enlarged and the Book of Remembrance installed in a new case. Each day a new page was turned and every Sunday the names of those killed in action in the corresponding week of the Second World War were read out. The College had not previously had a war memorial stone on which to lay wreaths and now a large stone was brought from the area near the Roman road at Blackpool Bridge in the Forest of Dean and set up on the grass to the east side of St George's chapel. A cross had been outlined on its upturned flat face and an inscription cut around its edge. The memorial was dedicated at the Remembrance Day Service on November 11th 1973.

In 1975 Padre Smith brought the college into contact with the Camphill Trust's Grange Village at Newnham. He had met Fraulein Erica Opitz in the garrison town of Krefeld. She, together with other protestant refugees from Nazi persecution, was living near Grange where they worked. The apprentices and staff gave much practical assistance and the chapel's congregation collected £300 towards a new multi-purpose building for the village. By way of thanks, Fraulein Opitz gave a pair of large and magnificent ceramic candlesticks for the chapel's altar.

On May 29th HRH Princess Margaret visited the college but St George's appeared only on the wet weather programme, as it had when HRH Princess Anne paid her visit on July 26th 1973. That autumn there came change with the arrival of two new chaplains with the same surname – the Reverends H L and A C Jones!

The army's priorities had always been military ones, but it seems curious that with the exception of one *Robot* report, the chaplains' notes seem to disappear from its pages for some years. There was however, note of a visit by the Chaplain-General, the Venerable Archdeacon P Mallet who celebrated Holy Communion, lunched with the churchwardens and Padre Smith and spent time with Padre Mears' House group.

The year 1982 saw the departure of the Reverend J Herve and the arrival of the Reverend H B Sherrington. It was stated in *The Robot* for that year that *"a Methodist took over from an Anglican, but the chapel did not fall down and the life of the church went on!"* In fact life seems to have become quite active and the new padre, as many of his predecessors had done before him, took stock and set about re-creating the chapel's spiritual life in his own way. Visiting preachers were invited to the beginning and end of term services and the Chaplain-General made an appearance. A Wednesday Club seems to have served the needs of staff children.

Religious education for the apprentices was divided between the three terms: the first introduced the whole field of religion; the second centred on the Christian faith; the third looked at how religion related to life. Courses frequently took place at the Royal Army Chaplains' Department at Bagshot Park, Surrey.

In 1983 the Remembrance Day Service was rendered all the more poignant by the recent conflict in the South Atlantic to regain the Falklands Islands, in which several former apprentices of the college had died. That year also saw the Diamond Jubilee of the college and there was a visit by HRH the Duchess of Gloucester on July 22nd. At the Jubilee service the preacher was the Reverend John Harris, the Vicar of Chepstow who was a former army chaplain.

It seems significant that with a Methodist padre, there should be a visit from the Deputy Chaplain-General, the Reverend Peter Whiting who was the senior Nonconformist Chaplain in the army. However, there was no mention in *The Robot* of St David's, the nonconformist army chapel. The academic year began, as usual with the Beachley Old Boys' reunion weekend and the chapel was full for the Sunday service. Later there was the Harvest Festival service which continued the tradition of displaying workshop "produce" alongside the usual fruit, vegetables and flowers. A rally by the local Methodist churches followed and later that year a candle-lit service of Nine Lessons and Carols was well attended by apprentices.

In the next few years both the college and *The Robot* went through changes and silence seems to have descended on the chapel but we do know that the Reverend Sherrington was succeeded by Major the Reverend R F Clayton-Jones, the Reverend Alun Price (who received an MBE for his service in the Gulf War) and the Reverend Roger Hall.

In 1987 three apprentices died in tragic circumstances and the parents and friends of one of them, Jonathon Peter Garnett, gave a

stained glass window to the chapel in his memory which was dedicated by the Chaplain-General. On Sunday June 12th, at the Beachley Old Boys' Association Service a second Book of Remembrance was also dedicated by the Chaplain-General. This commemorated those all those apprentices who had died whilst at the College.

1991 saw major renovation of the side chapel within St George's dedicated to the Beachley Old Boys' Association. It was repainted and re-carpeted. A new altar was made by a Mr Belcher of 88 Squadron in the workshops. At this time the Sunday School was flourishing, twenty- one apprentices were baptised and the Bishop of Tewkesbury, the Right Reverend G D J Walsh conducted the Confirmation Service. £1790 was collected at weekly services and given to a variety of charities.

One year later the Commandant, Colonel O W Haskell, announced in December 1992's *Robot* the news that the Apprentices' College was now approaching the end of its life and that training would cease during the summer of 1994. On Sunday February 27th 1994 a most poignant final service for the members of the Beachley Old Boy's Association took place. It was the culmination of the

Association's spectacular final College weekend. A moving final march-past through a dull wet Chepstow, an impressive and lengthy firework display in Chepstow Castle, and a sad Open Day in the camp culminated in a brave church parade with young and old together in the parade square. The service itself was rendered all the more poignant by the ceremonial, with young soldiers about to go out into an uncertain life in the army enacting an unforgettable ritual along-side their elders, many of whom had endured indescribable suffering in their young lives during various campaigns or as prisoners of war. Two Remembrance Books, in their cases, stood on either side below the chancel step and names were read out by an Old Boy and an Apprentice during the Act of Remembrance. The preacher was the Reverend Haydn L Jones, who gave a stunning sermon that left no one in doubt that the old values were still very much in many minds in the congregation. He was assisted by the last school chaplain, the Reverend W G Ashton. The chapel was crowded and the collection yielded £304.86.

Prior to the closure of the College an unusual ceremony took place at the 8.30 am assembly in the chapel. To quote the registers *"Assembly featured a public shaving and haircutting of Mr John Berryman, Burnham lecturer, in aid of UCH London where his daughter Ellen, is receiving treatment."*

The very last service of the Apprentices' College took place in the chapel on the second Sunday of Pentecost, June 5th 1994 with the Reverend Joe Rooney preaching. It was he who became the relief padre for the next seven years and went on to serve for a total of 29 years as an assistant padre, covering duties when the fifteen regular padres were away on duty with their battalions.

More than a year later, during which time there were significant structural changes within the camp to prepare for the arrival of an infantry battalion, the chapel's life was rekindled on Sunday December 6th, 1995 with a carol service for the 1st Battalion, The Royal Welsh Fusiliers. There was a congregation of three hundred and twenty. Thereafter the Reverend Richard Pluck seems to have had very small attendances but it must be borne in mind that an infantry battalion and its chaplain is often on standby or away from base. The following year on St David's Day, March 1st, 1996, however, the battalion was out in force with a congregation of three hundred and forty. On March 17th the Reverend Rooney dedicated an Army Cadet Force standard.

The pattern of camp life was now quite a different one, related to battalion and family life. There were many baptisms, the renewal of marriage vows and funerals. In January there was a funeral of three year old Keegan Lee Roberts, followed in the June by the dedication and planting of a cherry tree near the Chapel entrance as a memorial. Three hundred and four members of the battalion and their families attended the funeral service and one hundred and sixty-five the tree planting ceremony.

On Sunday September 6th 1998 five hundred and ninety five members of the newly arrived 1st Battalion the Cheshire Regiment and their families attended morning service to give thanks for their safe return from Northern Ireland. During the same month, on September 21st the Beachley Old Boys' Association held their Reunion service in the chapel after a considerable break. Thereafter they met annually. At the morning service on December 6th 1998, prayers were said for those members of the Cheshire Regiment killed by the Ballykelly bomb in 1982.

Weddings, renewal of marriage vows, baptisms of adults and children, and family memorial services continued whilst the registers reveal a regular attendance at Holy Communion Services. On October 19th 2000 a Drumhead Service was held to mark the arrival of the 2nd Battalion The Royal Anglian Regiment. There was a congregation of five hundred and high numbers also attended the subsequent Armistice and Carol services. Each regiment had its own customs and traditions and a regimental occasion, Sabroan day, also recorded a high attendance.

The following year the Reverend Peter Eagles arrived, his first service taking place on May 24th 2001. He reflected that although St George's Chapel remained spectacular and impressive, it was slightly impersonal and a gradual accumulation of regimental memorabilia would be welcome. He hoped that the Royal Anglians would be able to stay a little longer than previous battalions and leave more of a mark on the chapel. He also commented that it would be a sign of the fact that the church was the spiritual home of the resident battalion and it came to the fore particularly at times of significance, whilst parade services and weekly worship continued to take place regularly.

The Reverend David Moss, who from 2004 until 2007 was padre with the Green Howards, the 2nd Battalion the Yorkshire Regiment, described how the chapel was poorly attended until he organised Sunday services at 2.30pm, when the congregation consisting almost exclusively of Fijian servicemen attended quite regularly. He built the

The window to St Barbara, taken from the old chapel.
J Pullinger

congregation up from four to forty. In 2007 the 2nd Battalion Yorkshire Regiment (Green Howards) left and the 1st Battalion The Rifles arrived with a new policy that Beachley would be their base for some time. At that point the Ministry of Defence invested money in the chapel, aware that deployments overseas in Bosnia and Afghanistan were likely to place significantly greater demands on the chapel.

The current padre, the Reverend Chris Withers, described how there are now additional regular services held in St George's Chapel once a month for Fijian families from all over the area. There have been significant changes to the chapel since Beachley became the permanent home to the 450-500 personnel of the 1st Battalion the Rifles. It has been "personalised" and upgraded with the laying of a new carpet, raising of its own standards, decorations and the recording of significant occasions such as baptisms and memorials.

THE BUILDING

The new chapel was built near and to the south of the original converted barrack hut chapel on an untraditional south/north axis, presumably to use space economically at a time when many of the old huts were still in position and the whole College was being re-built. Designed in the Scandinavian style by Mr D Kearns, Chief Architectural Assistant to the then War Office, the building operations were directed by Mr J Richardson. Its steeply pitched roof is over 17 metres high and was originally sheathed in copper but subsequent leakage problems led to a complete re-cladding. The timber A-frames rest on low walls faced in Forest of Dean stone. The building is designed to feel spacious and open with the soaring roof as its main feature. The distinctive font, which was made by the apprentices at the Army Apprentices College, and altar reflect an elegant modern approach through their spare lines. However two of the windows from the old chapel have been skillfully incorporated into the building.

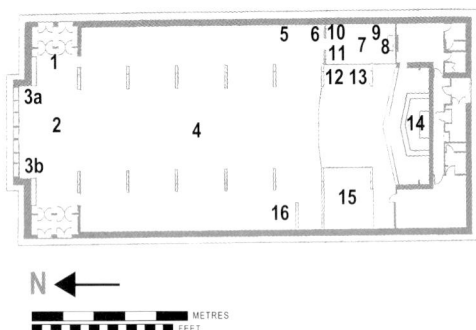

The Tour

Please note that the chapel is not normally accessible to members of the public and access is strictly by prior permission of the Ministry of Defence.

See figure 8 to follow the tour. Stand outside the chapel and note its steeply pitched roof. Near the entrance in the north wall is a cherry tree planted in memory of the three year old Keegan Lee Roberts, son of a Royal Welsh Fusilier. To the east surrounded by a lawn is the War memorial set in place during the College's Jubilee year, 1973 with the wording *"Use Well The Life For Which They Fought"*.

One enters the chapel through a **porch (1)** on the east side leading directly to a spacious assembly area with a light-giving glass and timber north wall containing a central door, matching porch and entrance on the west wall opposite and a polished timber floor. On the walls to the right are memorials to the members of 1st Battalion the Rifles who have died. Ahead **the font (2)** is an impressive sculptural feature with a Forest of Dean stone base designed rather like the reversed fins of a missile with the copper bowl cupped in the hollow at the top.

In the chapel's north wall are two **decorative memorial windows.** One **(3a)** is to Lieutenant-Colonel V T R Ford of the York and Lancaster Regiment who was the first Commandant of

The font made by the apprentices at the Army Apprentices' College at the time of the building of the new chapel to St George in 1963. *R Clammer*

the then Boys' Technical School from 1923 to 1927 and was considered to be its founder. The second **(3b)** is to Apprentice Tradesman Jonathon Peter Garnett who died from a brain tumour in 1987. His colleagues in 86 Training Squadron Royal Engineers donated the window in his memory.

Leaving this area, the main body of the church the **nave (4)** contains wooden pews made by successive groups of College apprentices and staff. Brass plates on the bench ends give the details. Few can deny that the timber trusses supporting the roof create an exceptional effect of space with light flooding in from the glass walls along the side aisles.

The fenestration is achieved by an abstract design of intersecting diagonal bars, apparently placed at random, holding largely clear glass. At designed interstices are stained glass panels in primary colours. The original intention was for coloured glass to be added as each senior group passed out of the Apprentices College but the tradition was not continued.

Standing in the nave, facing the altar, look up at the **flags** of the battalion and the central banner bearing the motto *"Once a Rifleman always a Rifleman... Fallen but not Forgotten"* which commemorates eight members of the Battalion recently killed in action, and was designed and presented by one of the families.

Moving towards the chancel, on the left on the East wall is a **brass memorial plate (5)** to Warrant Officer 1 Alfred Thomas Underwood BEM of the Royal Engineers and his wife Winifred. Known as Arthur by most of those who came into contact with him, his use of the cockney phrase of measurement *" 'arf a thou"* came to denote his skill on the lathe and hence his nickname. He is also remembered for being a Home Guard Instructor, a skilled maker of miniature field guns, and the man who hired out College sideshows for local fetes, especially during the fifties and sixties.

At the head of the eastern aisle to the left is a **Book of Remembrance (6)** of Riflemen killed in action. It is located just outside the wrought iron panels of **The Beachley Old Boys' Association** (BOBA) **chapel (7)**. The original architect's plan shows a much smaller chapel but a few months after its dedication it was enlarged to the current size. Its origin and the manufacture of the wrought iron panels are in themselves an interesting piece of Beachley history. The then Technical School padre, the Reverend JR Swift, obtained the design from an incurably ill patient he visited regularly in hospital, who sadly did not live to see the results of his ideas. The task of manufacture was given to 46B Group Blacksmiths, under Sergeant J Cleave, who completed the panels. They were finally installed by Sergeant A Jeffs, an Old Boy of the school. At the apex of the arch is the Association badge presented by 43 A and B groups in 1993.

In the BOBA chapel there are several items of interest. Behind the chapel's altar is a **stained glass window of St. George (8)** the patron. It was donated to the original old school chapel by members of the Beachley Old Boys' Association in 1957and moved to its present position when the new chapel was built. On the north wall above a fixed wall desk is a **brass plate (9)** commemorating the refurbishment and enlarging of the chapel in memory of Major-General P J Shears, Commandant of the College between 1935 and 1939. Originally there were two **Books of Remembrance (10 &11)** on display. The one which remains records the names of former Apprentices who were killed during the Second World War. It was donated from funds collected after the war and during the College's life a page was turned every day. The second was an alphabetical list of those who died whilst attending the Technical School or later College and is believed to be stored with the Beachley Old Boys Association records elsewhere.

Moving to the chancel step area, the **pulpit and adjacent lectern (12)**, formed from Forest stone are uncompromisingly Scandinavian design statements in keeping with the character of the whole chapel. Also in the chancel on the eastern roof truss is a **brass plate (13)** noting that a new chapel bell was given by members of the Beachley Old Boys' Association in May 1964. The bell hangs in the bell cote above and reputedly has a good tone.

The sanctuary is impressively lit by natural light from the sides and the large, simple cross above **the altar (14)** has concealed lighting behind it which creates an illusion that it is floating in front of the triangular wall. On the altar are **two crosses**, one of which is made from spent shell casings, and a **lamp** donated by Nordic House which is kept lighted at the gates when the battalion is on active service and extinguished only when the last soldier of the regiment returns to the base. A Bible for use in the sanctuary was given by Major A C Machin, the Royal Highland Fusiliers, an officer at the College whose memorial service took place on St Augustine's Day May 26th 1998. On the **sanctuary steps** are memorials to various servicemen, Lance-Corporal N R Joseph (1969), Lance-corporal Peter "Tinhead" Craddock (2006), Lance-Corporal Steven Sherwood, and O P Herrick (2005).

The altar, showing the lamp on the left which is kept allght outside the gates until all the personnel deployed overseas have safely returned. On the right is a candle stick made of spent shell cases.
R Clammer

To the right of the altar is a hanging **censor** from the old chapel and nearby the **organ (15)** which was installed during 1971 and was dedicated on November 7th by the Bishop of Gloucester. It was designed by K F Prior and built by Messrs. Rushworth and Dreaper of Liverpool. Installation of the instrument presented many problems due to the unusual architectural features of the chapel, particularly from the acoustic point of view. In order to use the space as effectively as possible, the pipework and the blower mechanism, together with the swell box have been grouped to the right of the chancel, looking towards the altar. The console is linked to the organ proper by a system of electric cables and relays, so that the keyboard action is extremely light and flexible. The organ fits neatly between two of the roof trusses and is concealed by an open screen constructed of vertical wooden rails whose alignment creates a chevron pattern echoing the pitch of the roof.

Returning once more to the nave and before leaving, note the partition in the west aisle which contains a back-lit **stained glass window of St. Barbara (16)**, who is the patron saint of people who work with explosives such as artillery men, and miners. It also came from the old chapel and was originally presented by the members of the Army Technical School in 1957. Both St Barbara and St. George flanked the altar in the old building and thus maintain the connection between the old and the new. Along the side walls are the colourful regimental shields.

Near the exit there are **boards (17)** listing the baptisms taken place in the chapel and also a list of the padres. Finally above the lobby and immediately ahead is the striking **stained glass window of Saint Alban (18)** who was a Roman soldier based in Britain when

Christianity was outlawed. Despite this, Alban gave shelter to a Christian priest and was so impressed by his faith that he converted to Christianity. He became the first Christian martyr in Britain when he was killed for not only harbouring a Christian but being one himself. Commissioned by the Devonshire and Dorset Regiment for the Munster Garrison church in West Germany, it was designed by the artist Juliet Pannett, whose husband served in the regiment. It was removed from that church when it was deconsecrated and was in the garrison church in Osnabruck until it moved to Beachley in November 2010 where it remains as part of the Rifles' heritage.

This stained glass window of St Alban in St George's Chapel. *R Clammer*

13 THE CHURCH OF THE SACRED HEART, SEDBURY

HISTORY

Not until 1939 was there a permanent Roman Catholic Church east of the river Wye in the Tidenham area. Prior to that the nearest was in Welsh street, Chepstow, where the first Roman Catholic church was built in 1827, later superseded by St Mary's in Bulwark. From 1930 until 1937 the growing congregation in the Tidenham parish area had been administered to at the Army Technical School by Father Andrew Waters and for the following two years by Canon F Ryan. An extract from a communication from Bishop William Lee to Father Michael O Ryan dated 20th June 1939, after praising work done by the Fathers of the Order of the Oblates of Mary Immaculate at Kingswood who were the body in charge, runs as follows: *"To my mind you ought to have the parish of Coleford and with a third Mass centre at Lydney. Your fathers would have ample score for their zeal and energy... The priest of Coleford is Chaplain to the Beachley Camp where there are about one hundred catholic boys."* Later there were services in the school hall in Sedbury in buildings which were possibly the Junior Mixed School and also in the Warrant Officers' and Sergeants' Mess which was located on a site next to the current post office at Sedbury.

The first Roman Catholic Church of the Sacred Heart was opened in a disused military hut on Grahamstown Road at Sedbury in 1939.
Courtesy of the late Father Fanning

The new Church of the Sacred Heart at Sedbury was established in 1939, largely through the efforts of Father J J Donohue, in a building at the end of Grahamstown Road, Sedbury, formerly used to house shipyard workers and prisoners of war during the First World War. During the Second World War the local congregation was joined by German prisoners-of-war billeted nearby who did much to beautify its interior. The approach to the church in the 1940s was between high barbed wire fences through which the prisoners' colourful and creative gardens could be seen to brighten an otherwise grim setting.

By 1976 the church was deteriorating badly and was becoming unsuitable for the growing community of Sedbury, which had expanded rapidly after the War. An appeal to raise funds entitled "The Lovers of the Sacred Heart" was launched by the priest Father Fanning and met with an immediate and splendid response. The adjoining site was bought by the Fathers of the Oblates of Mary Immaculate and the building of the new church began.

The consecration was conducted by Bishop Alexander of Clifton on June 1st 1988. Father Fanning continued to serve the church for many years thereafter until his reluctant retirement in 2006 at the age of 89 when the Parishes of Sedbury and Coleford were transferred to the Clifton Diocese based in Bristol and became part of the large Catholic parish of St Margaret Mary, centred on Coleford, within the Roman Catholic Diocese of Clifton. The church of the Sacred Heart is now served by a Diocesan Priest who lives in the presbytery previously occupied by Father Fanning.

THE BUILDING

In the nineteenth century new Catholic churches, in common with those of the other Christian denominations were in a variety of styles, from classical Byzantine, and Romanesque through to the phases of Gothic. The twentieth century, however, saw the Catholic Church

The Church of the Sacred Heart at Sedbury.
R Clammer

venturing into more adventurous architectural waters and Clifton Cathedral stands at the forefront of modern design. The Sacred Hearts, though on a far more modest scale, reflects much of the same innovative style, being a steel-framed building with the great pyramid-like slate roof covering the whole floor plan.

The consecration of the new Church of the Sacred Heart on June 1st 1988 by Bishop Alexander of Clifton.
Courtesy of the late Father Fanning

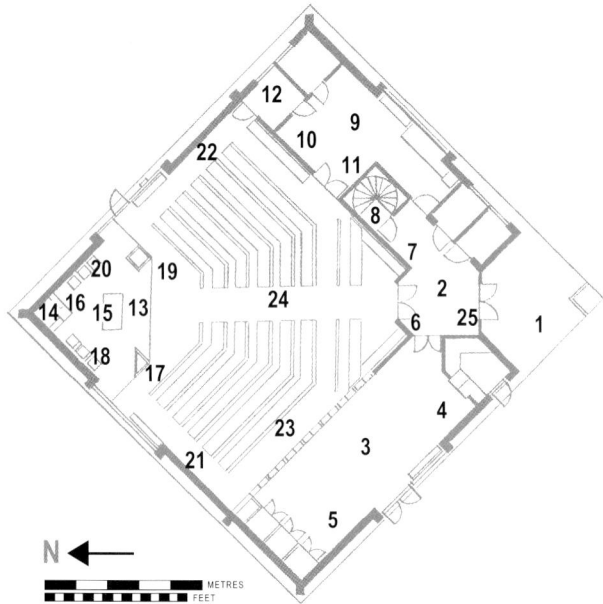

Fig. 9 The Church of the Sacred Heart, Sedbury

THE TOUR

Figure 9 accompanies this tour. The **entrance (1)** is in the southern corner via an open-sided covered loggia leading into a **narthex (2)** or lobby. From this doors open on the south west side into the meetings room or **vestibule (3)** containing the **statues of St Theresa (4) and St Anthony (5)**. Its south eastern wall is a timber and glass screen through which the Nave and Sanctuary can be clearly seen.

Back in the lobby is the **Dedication stone (6)** and the original **wooden crucifix (7)** that hung in the old church, its Christ figure carved with penknives by German prisoners-of-war, many of whom are buried in the war graves cemetery, next to St John's churchyard at Beachley.

On the south eastern side of the church are the stairs to the **upper gallery (8)** and the **sacristy** containing **the original brass tabernacle (9) wooden altar frontal (10)** and **another crucifix (11)** from the original church. The **confessional (12)** opens off the same room.

Raised on a dias is the **Sanctuary** area **(13)**. An oxidised silver **tabernacle (14)** depicting the last Supper stands behind the **altar (15)** whilst above hangs a large **Christ figure (16)** with arms open in welcome, crowning the composition. On the altar is another oxidised

silver **crucifix (15)**, flanked by matching candlesticks and an altar frontal bearing a nativity scene. On the dais to the left is the wooden **pulpit (17)** adjacent to a painted **figure of St Joseph (18)** while to the right is **the font (19)** and the **figure of St Mary (20)**.

Around the walls of the nave are the **Stations of the Cross (21 & 22)** all in oxidised silver. Above the screen to the north west are **framed embroideries (23)** by parishioner Mrs Ivy Webb, in memory of her husband who was lost at sea. Returning through the **Nave (24)** with its solid and cleverly angled pews, look above the entrance doors at a gallery. As you leave the building, above the outer entrance doors and within the foyer is a **figure of Jesus (25) revealing the Sacred heart** and a nearby ornamental oxidised silver **Holy Water Stoup** on the wall.

The statues are a reminder that all statuary and sculpture in ancient churches was painted, often in very bright colours and that the iconoclasm brought about by the Reformation of the churches robbed us of a wealth of mediaeval art. The church is an interesting fusion of the old and the new, and there is a feeling of continuity.

Please note that the church is kept locked and under surveillance. Please contact the Sacristan if wishing to visit the church.

Ordnance Survey Grid reference SHEET 162 scale 1:50 000 : 546939

The worship area of Sedbury Evangelical Church at Christmas 2013. *R Clammer*

14 SEDBURY EVANGELICAL CHURCH

HISTORY

Before the First World War the area between Beachley and Tutshill was largely agricultural farmland or marsh with a farm at Pennsylvania and sporadic cottages. Children went to the school either at Tutshill or Beachley. Sedbury as a community emerged mostly as a result of the First World War when barracks were rapidly put up to house prisoners-of-war and for troops of the Royal Engineers, brought in to build the National Shipyard No. 2 at Beachley. The billets were mostly located at the end of Grahamstown Road with others in and around King Alfred's Road. After the War the prisoner-of-war camp was moth-balled behind its wire fence. However, the arrival of the Army Boys' Technical School at Beachley in 1924 brought in more service and civilian personnel, who needed to be housed and their children educated in the area. As a consequence gradually more properties were built at Pennsylvania (now Mercian Way). Children went to school in a converted army hut on King Alfred's Road which is now Sedbury Community Centre.

With the onset of the Second World War the army huts at Grahamstown Road were brought into use once more, providing accommodation for both prisoners-of-war and army personnel and used as workshops and machine shops. One Tidenham Historical Group member recalls as a small boy visiting his grandmother on Grahamstown Road, looking through the high wire fencing around the camp and admiring the beautiful gardens created by the German prisoners-of-war.

When the war was over, the buildings were no longer used and the army camp gradually became derelict once again. Seeing the opportunity to get yet more use from the buildings, the government converted some into accommodation to assist with the housing shortage of de-mobbed service personnel. Others were demolished to make way for new housing. The increase in population was significant and in 1951 a group of people including Mr Williams and the Misses Roberts of Day House Farm decided to set up Sedbury Mission (as it

Sedbury
Evangelical
Church was
opened in 1951
with a particular
emphasis on
providing activities
for children and
young people.
R Clammer

was then known) in one of the disused army buildings with the primary purpose of providing local services and activities for young people. These were organised by Mr and Mrs Nicholas from Bristol and one end of the building was converted for use as their accommodation, the main meeting hall being in the other part of the hut.

The church was extremely active with a six-class Sunday school, a youth club which met on Thursday evenings and a women's group called "Happy Hour" which met on Tuesday afternoons. One local resident recalled how at the age of about eight he attended the church, the youth club and the church outings. He especially remembered that on one occasion three coach loads of children and adults left Sedbury for Barry.

In 1942, Sedbury Park became the location of an Approved School for Boys. After the opening of Sedbury Mission the lads were marched in line through Sedbury with their teacher Mr Tarrant to attend a service once a month until the school closed in 1986.

In 1984 following a complete refurbishment, the name Sedbury Mission was changed to Sedbury Evangelical Church. Nowadays the young people's ethos still continues with regular weekly meetings of the Churches Together youth group as well as regular services and bible meetings. The story comes full circle with the interesting and curious fact that the founder of one of the "youngest" churches in Tidenham Parish was a farmer who worked land at Lancaut, the location of our oldest recorded church dating from 625 AD!

THE BUILDING

The design and orientation of this church was pre-determined by its origin as a war-time building. With a new roof, walls, windows, and exterior pebble-dash coating, it has been transformed into a warm and comfortable place of worship. The main entrance at the northern end of the building on Grahamstown Road leads into a lobby from which doors lead into the main body of the church. The restored roof beams are clearly visible. Individual seats provide flexibility in the layout of the room. At the far end is a wooden lectern, a table, organ and raised dais, behind which is an attractive light pine clad wall bearing the words *"Jesus Christ is Lord"* in blue.

To the right of the dais a doorway opens onto a short flight of steps leading down into a comfortable meeting room with informally arranged chairs, tables and a small library. A kitchen area with a servery leads off the meeting room.

Ordnance Survey Grid reference SHEET 162 scale 1:50 000: 546939

An aerial view of all three chapels at the Army Apprentices' College Beachley in 1969. The single steep roof-line of the Anglican Chapel of St George can be seen nearest to the Severn Bridge. The flat-roofed rectangular building with four distinctive vertical rows of small windows and one row of slightly larger windows nearer the foreground by the playing fields is St David's Non-Conformist chapel. The multi-facetted roof-line of St Joseph's Roman Catholic chapel with its distinctive cross can be seen towards the right of the picture.
Robot magazine

15 ST JOSEPH'S ROMAN CATHOLIC CHAPEL, THE ARMY APPRENTICES' COLLEGE, BEACHLEY

HISTORY

The short life of this little catholic chapel, opened in 1969, seems to have left few official records and scarcely any history. It was built at a time when a wave of optimism for the future of the Army Apprentices' College had inspired a considerable rebuilding programme on the peninsular. While the first Severn Bridge was still rising above the demolished army huts that had once been the barrack rooms, new accommodation was springing up, to include three chapels.

St Joseph's was built in the north east corner of the "roman" grid of the camp, on the site of the old NAAFI building and cinema. Its altar was in the west of the chapel, contrary to tradition. It came within the catholic parish of St Mary Margaret based on Coleford, in the Diocese of Clifton.

There is speculation that the dedication to St Joseph may have paid tribute to the notion of his role as the foster father of Jesus and therefore of the young apprentices who worshipped in the chapel. The consecration took place on February 9th 1969 and was conducted by the Right Reverend Gerard W Tickle, Bishop-in-Ordinary to the forces. The chaplains were Father Liam Fanning and Father J Halpin.

The Roman Catholic chapel of St Joseph at the Army Apprentices' College, Beachley built in 1969 and photographed shortly before its demolition in late 1999.
A T Underwood

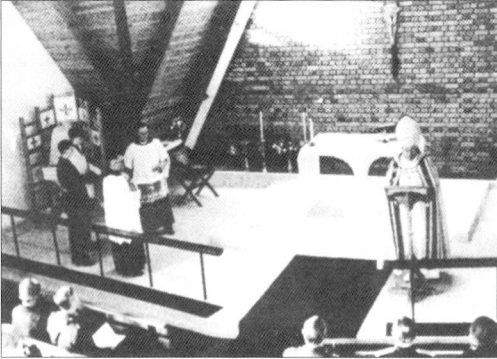

The consecration service in 1969 of the chapel of St Joseph at Beachley Army Apprentices' College conducted by the Right Reverend Gerard W Tickle, Bishop-in-Ordinary to the Armed Forces showing the sculptural altar. *Robot magazine*

On July 5th 1984 a Requiem Mass took place for Mrs Joan Kirkham, the wife of former College Regimental Sergeant Major, George Kirkham, Grenadier Guards. Although a practising Catholic, she had been the much respected and loved caretaker of St George's Church of England chapel at the Apprentices' College. On retirement her husband had become a member of the Queen's Bodyguard of Yeoman based at St James Palace and his portrait hung in the Royal British Legion in Chepstow.

With the closure of the Army Apprentices College in 1994 and the arrival of successive Infantry Battalions, the chapel was found to be surplus to requirements and was finally demolished between November 1999 and January 2000. Of the fittings to survive some items went to St George's and others, including the organ, went to St Mary's Roman Catholic Church at Bulwark, Chepstow. Father Rooney described how the books from the chapel were boxed up and sent to Africa.

THE BUILDING

Unhappily it is now only possible to tour the chapel via the original architect's plan, engineer's drawings which survive on microfiche, and photographs. It is through these that it is possible to appreciate the inventive structure of the building and examine it in detail.

Architecturally more adventurous, hexagonal in plan, and with its roof reaching to the ground, its design preceded that of the Roman Catholic Church of the Sacred Heart at Sedbury and that of St Mary's Roman Catholic Church in Bulwark, Chepstow. The chapel's architect was D Kearns, the chief architectural assistant with the Ministry of Public Building for the War Office who had also been responsible for St George's chapel. The designer was F B Minter and the consulting Structural Engineer was P H Robinson, BSc (Eng). The plans were prepared between June 1965 and April 1967. The structure of the building was of laminated timber main roof beams, as in St George's, but the hexagonal structure required a more complex assembly.

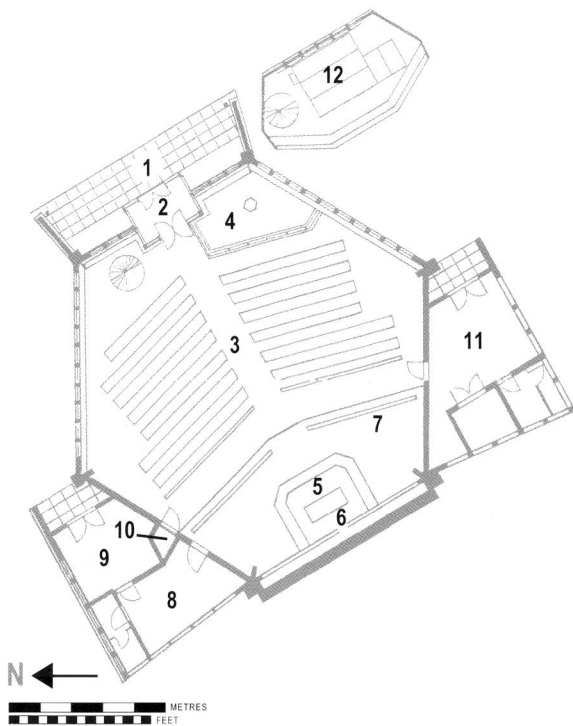

Fig. 10 Chapel of St Joseph, Beachley Barracks

Figure 10 shows the floor plan of the building and accompanies the "virtual" tour.

The chapel was approached from the north east, where in the centre of the broad covered **loggia (1)**, the outer and inner doors of the **porch (2)** led to the spacious, centrally planned **nave (3)**. To the left was the baptistry where the hexagonal **font (4)** stood. The central aisle, between pews angled to face the sanctuary, led to the **altar (5),** an open sculptural form that seemed reminiscent of a shrine. Behind, on a fair-faced brick wall hung a naturalistic **figure of Christ on the cross (6)**. To the south east within the altar-rail of the Sanctuary, apparently stood the **tabernacle (7)** while the candelabra and flower vases stood behind the table of the altar ranged along the foot of the wall on a raised shelf.

To the right of the altar a door led from the sanctuary into the **clergy vestry (8)** from which the priest could enter into the working **vestry (9)**. **The confessional (10)** opened from the nave. To the south east of the nave a door opened into the **guild room (11)** where staff and apprentices' groups could meet. At each corner of the hexagonal pyramid that formed the chapel the triangular interstices between the plain solid walls were of timber match boarding behind the diagonal main beams. Above the entrance porch was the **organ and choir gallery (12)**, reached by a freestanding spiral staircase. The floors of the sanctuary and the recessed baptistery were of buff terrazzo, whilst those of the nave and other public areas were covered in more serviceable lino. The porches were tiled.

The Free Church Chapel of St David at The Army Apprentice's College, Beachley was consecrated in June 1969 by the Deputy Chaplain-General, the Reverend D H Witford.
A T Underwood

16 THE FREE CHURCH CHAPEL OF ST DAVID, ARMY APPRENTICES' COLLEGE, BEACHLEY

HISTORY

Although the Anglican chapel of St George was the main focus for the spiritual life of The Army Technical School, the Royal Army Chaplain's Department provided padres of all denominations. The needs of what the army termed ODs (Other Denominations) were administered to by the Reverend David Owen, the Moderator of the Monmouth Presbytery. A letter in the *Robot* of February 1944 is interesting: *"Dear Padre, I wish to express my sincere appreciation to the School Commandant for making it possible for me to meet all the members of the Presbyterian Church and to arrange for them in the future a 'Young Communicants' class ', with a view to church membership. By what I saw and heard, parents can be very happy in the thought that the spiritual welfare of the boys is well cared for. I was very happy at the response of the Presbyterians".*

On May 18th 1944 *The Robot* reported that a unique service in the annals of the Army Technical School had been held, at which fifteen Presbyterian Tradesmen were admitted to full membership of the church. It is unclear where the non-conformist services were held but probably St Georges' chapel served all denominations.

On June 8th 1969, in what had now become the Army Apprentices' College, the new Chapel of St David was opened by the Deputy Chaplain-General, the Reverend D H Witford. It provided all the Non-Conformist denominations with a worthy place of worship. Later that year the Reverend David Owen was guest speaker at a combined morning service at St George's Anglican chapel. At its close he was presented with a rose bowl as a token of the appreciation of the Army Apprentices College for his thirty years of ministry as a chaplain to the Church of Scotland and Presbyterian congregations. *The Robot* reported that few could

The retirement presentation ceremony to Rev. Owen 16th November 1969 when he left St David' chapel, the Army Apprentices College, Beachley. *Robot magazine*

The interior of the Free Church Chapel of St David at the Army Apprentices College, Beachley in 1973.
Robot magazine

have spoken to Padre Owen for more than a few minutes without catching something of the inner faith and love for his fellow men radiated by his quiet, but unfailingly cheerful personality. He died on May 27th 1971 and was remembered with gratitude and affection by the many who had benefited from his friendship and counsel.

Padre Alan Spivey then arrived to administer to the Church of Scotland, the Baptist, the Presbyterian, the Methodist and the Congregational members of the College. He worked as the second chaplain, in conjunction with Padre Spilman. By August 1970 the OD club had been formed, a youth club which, judging from the tone of Padre Spivey's comment that *"nothing of great consequence has yet happened!"*, was anticipated to have one or two lively nights.

In the spring of 1975 the Reverend P A Mears made a significant contribution to the Padre's notes in *The Robot*. He seems to have re-organised the routine at St David's chapel in a gesture aimed at making the worship more meaningful for the apprentices. A four-weekly pattern of Sunday services was initiated. On the first Sunday there was a Holy Communion service, re-written to be more intelligible, which was attended by an average of ten communicants. On the second

Sunday was an "Interview" service aimed at keeping in touch with the modern media approach. A visiting speaker having a particular skill, expertise or experience was central to the service. A volunteer Samaritan came, as did a nun with three unmarried mothers from her shelter. The third Sunday was devoted to music, with Christian groups like *The Fishers* performing. The fourth Sunday was a family service along the traditional Free Church lines but with the emphasis on informality. All this was in conjunction with a religious education programme, community service projects and a youth club.

By 1995 when a regiment had replaced the Army Apprentices College, St. David's had been closed. It is now the site of a gym.

THE BUILDING

A photograph of the chapel shows a flat-roofed, functional, rectangular building with ceiling to floor windows and a large cross on the outer wall. The interior view taken in 1973 shows a simple arrangement of chairs, a raised dais with a simple table or altar and a raised cross strikingly placed on a plain wall. Other decoration was minimal.

tidenham historical group

Tidenham Historical Group meets on a regular basis to discuss and share information on the history of the area, whilst undertaking research on specific small projects. We are a group of interested residents who are keen to ensure that aspects of local history are recorded and not lost. If you have information such as photographs or documents about the local area which you would like to share with us or would like to join the group please use the contact details below:

website: www. tidenhamhistory.co.uk
e-mail: info@tidenhamhistory.co.uk
tel : 01291 623736 or 01291 621694

ACKNOWLEDGEMENTS

Many people were involved in the research, writing and publication of this book. The willingness to share information and the interest in the book itself has been extremely gratifying. The group would like to thank everyone for their help whether it was with researching and writing the chapters, supplying illustrations, providing information, book production or welcoming us into their buildings. It sincerely apologises to anyone inadvertently omitted below from the list of those who have contributed over the years.

Christie Arno, W. S. Atkins, David and Janet Barber, Pat Barrett, Beachley Old Boy's Association, Keith Bergum, Gerald Blunt, Mary Bruton, Chepstow Museum, Carol and Richard Clammer, Rev. Canon Tom Clammer, Bob Cook, Gerald Davies, The Gloucester Diocese, Rev. Peter Eagles, Hazel Evans, the late Rose Evans, the late Father Liam Fanning, John Furley, Ian and Fiona Gardiner, Gloucestershire Archives, Sarah-Jane Gilchrist, Rev. Canon Royston Grosvenor, Malcolm Hay, M and L Hollies, the late Anthony James, Barbara Jones, Avril Kear, Margaret Kinsey, Alan Kittridge, Christine Leighton, Jen Van Loon, Liz and Gerald McBride, G Mead, Rev. David Moss, The National Lottery, Father Barnabas Page, Charles Parry, Mr Payne, Sue Pears, L Phillips, Liz Pitman, John and the late Joyce Pullinger, Anne Rainsbury, Pastor Chris and HoSoon Rees, Johnne Roy, Severn Area Rescue Association, Elder Tony Samuel, Kate Samuel-Birt, Rev. Janet Taylor, Tidenham Parochial Church Council, Rev. David Treharne, Keith Underwood, Mrs Audrey Vaughan, Carol Voyce, the late Mercedes and Linda Walters, Mr Webb, Padre Chris Withers, Allan White, Joy Wright.

BIBLIOGRAPHY

A History of the County of Gloucester: Volume 10: Westbury and Whitstone Hundreds, 1972

Archaeologica: Or Miscellaneous Tracts Relating to Antiquity, Society of Antiquarians, London, 1841

Badminton Monuments, National Library of Wales, Aberwystwyth

Barnes, Capt. D and Thomas, Major D. *The Story of the Army Apprentices' College, Chepstow* 1923-83, Beachley, 1983

Bradney, Sir Joseph. *A History of Monmouthshire Vol. 4 Part 1 The Hundred of Caldicot,* Merton Priory Press, 1994

Cooke, Arthur. *The Forest Of Dean*

Cook, Bob. *Record Of Beachley Churchyard Graves,* (unpublished) 1995

Craster, O. E. *Tintern Abbey,* HMSO, 1965

Duthie, Arthur Louis. *Decorative Glass Processes,* Constable, 1908/1919

Ecclesiology Today, Journal of the Ecclesiology Society 25 April, 2001

Elrington & Herbert, *The Victoria County History of the Counties of England. A History of Gloucestershire Vol. 10,* University of London, 1972

English Romanesque Art, Catalogue to the Arts Council of Great Britain Exhibition at the Hayward Gallery, London 5 April- 8, Wedenfield and Nicholson, July 1984

Fanning, Fr. L. *Dedication Booklet And Order Of Service,* June 1st 1988

Fendley, John Ed. *Notes on the Diocese of Gloucester, by Chancellor Richard Parsons c1700,*Vol 19 Gloucester Record Series, The Bristol and Gloucestershire Archaeological Society, 2005

Findlay, Donald. *Report For The Council For The Care Of Churches,* 13 Jan, 1995

Fraser, A. *The Lives of the Kings and Queens of England,* Weidenfield & Nicholson, 1975

Gandy, Walter. *The Romance of Glass-Making,* 1898

Grigson, G. *England's Smallest Parish?* Country Life Magazine October 30th, 1954

Historical, Monumental and Genealogical Collections Relative to the County of Gloucester, printed from the original Papers of Ralph Bigland Vol 3, Gloucester City Library

Hadley, Dr. Dennis. *Window Cash Book*

Hart, Dr. Cyril. *Dean Archaeology No.2,* 1982

Hart, Dr. Cyril. *Dean Archaeology* No.3, 1990

The Hockaday Abstracts 1844, Gloucester County Records Office

Hockaday Records, Gloucester County Record Office trans. Bristol & Gloucestershire Arch. Society No 106, 1988

Johnson, Paul. *A History of Christianity*, Penguin, 1978

Jordan, Christopher. *Severn Enterprise,* Arthur Stockwell, 1977

Kelly's Directory Gloucester, Gloucester County Records Office, 1856, 1932,1935

Kissack, Keith. *Monmouth The Making Of A Town,* Phillimore, 1975

Lefebve, Dom Gaspar. *Duntisbourne Rouse:* Gloucestershire Magazine, June 12, 2012

Mead, G. *The People of Tidenham* (unpublished), 1983

Mills, Rosie. Ed. *Ely Gallery Guide:* The Stained Glass Museum, 2007

Mingay, G. E. *Rural Life In Victorian England*, Lund Humphries, 1976

Molesworth, N. D, *Sculpture in England – Medieval*, British council 1951

Morgan, F. C. *The Herefordshire School of Sculpture and Kilpeck Church,* 2nd Edition, 1958

Morris, John. Ed. *Domesday Book,* Phillimore, 1982

Parry, Charles. *A Survey of St James' Church, Lancaut, Gloucestershire* Bristol & Gloucestershire Archaeological Society Vol 108, 1990

Proud, Linda. *Christianity in England,* Pitkin, 1978

Pullinger, J. *Boughspring Roman Villa*

Ormerod, George. *Sedbury Park Roman Remains*

Ormerod, George. *Strigulensia,* 1861

Robinson, David. M. *Tintern Abbey,* Cadw, 1995

The Wesleyan Chapel Committee. *Returns of Accommodation provided in Wesleyan Methodist Chapels and Other Preaching Places*, Wesleyan Conference Office, London, 1875

Tidenham Parish Magazine

The Robot, The Journal of the Army Apprentices' College, Nov 1924-1983

The Lancaut Preservation Group. *The Church of St. James at Lancaut,* The Crickley Hill Archaeological Trust and the Gloucestershire Heritage Trust, 1985

Tredegar Park Monuments in Post Mortem 1634-35, National Library of Wales

Trevelyan, G. M. *Illustrated English Social History,* Longmans, Green & Co., 1951

Verey & Brooks. *Buildings of England: Gloucestershire 2; The Vale & Forest of Dean,* Yale, 2002

Victoria County History Vol X: Gloucestershire, Oxford University Press, 1972

Vidler, Alec. R. *The Church in an Age of Revolution,* Penguin Pelican, 1977

Wakeman. *Observations on the Town & Castle of Chepstow,* Journal of the British Archaeological Association Vol 10, 1855

Wallace, Robert. Ed. *Eleanor Ormerod, Economic Entomologist, Autobiography and Correspondence,* John Murray, 1904

Waters, Ivor. *Beachley: Between The Wye And The Severn,* The Printing Club
    Of The Army Apprentices' College Chepstow 1977
Waters, Ivor. *About Chepstow,* Newport and Monmouthshire branch of the
    Historical Association and the Chepstow Society, 1952
Welander, David. *The Stained Glass of Gloucester Cathedral,* 1985
Williams, David. H. *The Welsh Cistercians Cyoeddiadau Sisterciaidd,* 1984 Vol
    1&11, Gracewing, 2001
Wright, Eileen. *A History of Stroat Mission 1889-1989*
Zarnecki, George. *English Romanesque Lead Sculpture,* Tiranti, 1957

OTHER SOURCES
1902 Ordinance Survey Map, Alan Godfrey Maps, Leadgate, Consett
Bristol Mercury Newspaper
Chepstow Weekly Advertiser Newspaper records, Chepstow Museum
Clifton Diocesan Archives (Coleford File)
Gloucester Archives
The Gloucestershire Citizen Newspaper
Gloucester Diocesan Records
Sedbury Evangelical Church member records and website
Stroat Evangelical Church archive collection
The Gwent Archives, Ebbw Vale
The Monmouthshire Beacon Newspaper, Chepstow Library Collection
The Poyntz Family Records
The Register of Services of St George's Chapel Jan78-Sept 2001
Thornborrow, Philip. *Wesleyan Chapels the 1873 returns,* My Wesleyan
    Methodists website - (mywesleyanmethodists.org.uk)
Tidenham Historical Group records
Tidenham Parish Church website - (tidenhamparishchurch.co.uk)
Tidenham Parish Records, Gloucester County Record Office (With the
    permission of the Tidenham with Lancaut and Beachley Parochial
    Church Council.)
Western Daily Press, Newspaper 1888
Woodcroft Christian Centre website - (woodcroft-online.org.uk)

APPENDIX ONE

ST LUKE'S CHURCH MEMORIALS

As you enter the south door, on the wall of the porch is a plaque:

THE PARISH OF TIDENHAM
SUPPORTED TWO FAMILIES OF BELGIAN REFUGEES
FROM OCTOBER 1914-MAY 1916
ONE OF THEM, LOUIS DELAUVER,
EXECUTED THE CARVING OF THE PANELS ON THE EAST WALL
WHICH WERE PLACED THERE BY EVELYN SEYS WIDOW
AS AN ACT OF THANKSGIVING TO GOD
FOR THE PRESERVATION OF HER SONS
DURING THE GREAT WAR

As you enter the church, on the left on the West wall is a brass plaque:

TO THE GLORY OF GOD
AND IN LOVING MEMORY OF
STANHOPE STOTT-STANHOPE
THE ELECTRIC LIGHT WAS INSTALLED
IN THIS CHURCH BY HIS WIDOW
ANNIE STOTT-STANHOPE
MAY 1925

To the left of the first arch over the nave hangs a printed roll of honour to the dead of the First World War with 208 names and the heading:

ROLL OF HONOUR FOR THE PARISHES OF TIDENHAM & BEACHLEY
1914-1919
PRO REGE ET PATRIA

Beneath the window to the right hand side of the west wall is inscribed:

TO THE GLORY OF GOD
AND IN LOVING MEMORY OF
HILDA MARY MILOREND AND
JOHN LANCELOT LINDHAM
THIS WINDOW WAS ERECTED OCT. 1894

Beneath the window on the North Wall depicting St Matthew is the inscription:

To the Glory of God and in memory of
CHARLES JAMES LINDHAM & MARY his wife

The bottom of the window on the North wall, showing St Luke, is inscribed:

To the Glory of God and in memory of
Beatrice Elizabeth Jones 1894-1967

Under the window on the north wall, near to the vestry is a brass plaque:

To the glory of God
And in loving memory of
CAPT. ARTHUR TALBOT RNR

To the left and right of the altar are two large wooden panels. That on the left is inscribed:

TO THE GLORY OF GOD
AND IN UNDYING HONOUR AND GRATITUDE
TO THE MEN OF THE PARISH OF TIDENHAM
WHO GAVE THEIR LIVES FOR THEIR KING AND COUNTRY
IN THE GREAT WAR

THOMAS LESLIE ADAMS	WILLIAM JAMES HOWELL
WILLIAM GEORGE ANDREWS	LEONARD REECE HOWELL
SYDNEY HOWARD ANTHONY	IVOR JENKINS
EDGAR JOSEPH ARNOLD	WILLIAM KELLY
HENRY JAMES BALL	EDWARD PATRICK KEOGH
CHARLES BATTS	JOHN KING
ALBERT WALTER BLATCHLEY	ROBERT NORMAN
W. H. BROWN	JAMES ALBERT POWELL
GEORGE FREDERICK BROOKS	FRANK REEKS
WILLIAM GEORGE CORNWALL	JESSE REEKS
WILLIAM SYDNEY DAVEY	JAMES ALFRED SANDFORD
HAROLD THORNE EDWARDS	JAMES THOMAS
JOHN JAMES ELLIS	JOHN TURNER
HOWARD WILLIAM ENGLISH	ALBERT HENRY TYLER
THOMAS HENRY GROVES	GEORGE VICTOR VICKERY
HARRINGTON EUGENE HAMMOND	JOHN WILLIAM YOUNG

The choir stalls on the north side of the chancel are inscribed:
TO THE GLORY OF GOD
AND IN MEMORY OF
MABEL EDITH MARY FRANCIS
OF EAST CLIFF
1891-1957

The base of the first window on the south wall after turning right on entering the church by the south door is inscribed with:
To the glory of God and in loving memory of
John Frank Cyril Grace & Ruth Armstrong

Under the second window on the south wall is inscribed:
IN MEMORY OF CATHERINE WIDOW OF
JOHN CAMPBELL ESQ.CAPTAIN RMLI
DIED NOV.5 1880 IN HER 81ST YEAR

MEMORIALS IN ST.LUKE'S ROOM
On the inside of the main door to St Luke's room:
PRESENTED BY
SIR HOLBURT WARING
IN MEMORY OF
SIR HAROLD
AND LADY WINIFRED WARING

Below the window on the north wall are three memorials:
DAVID VERNON FLOYD
25.6.23-18.8.90
PCC MEMBER
SO THAT ALL MAY SHARE HIS LIGHT

IN LOVING MEMORY OF
SARAH LOVELL
NEE GLENDENNING
DIED ON 3rd AUGUST 1993

IN MEMORY OF MUCH
LOVED AUNT & GODMOTHER
NORA LOUISE
FOURACRE
1909-1994

Under the left hand window of the east wall:

IN FOND MEMORY OF

A LOVING FATHER

WILLIAM HENRY

VALE

1909-1994

On the east door:

GIVEN IN MEMORY OF

ELSIE GRACE

1903-1981

AND

FRANCIS CHARLES BRADSHAW

1897-1993

Below the right hand window in the east wall:

IN FOND MEMORY OF

A DEVOTED MOTHER

GWENDOLINE ANNIE

VALE

1904-1994

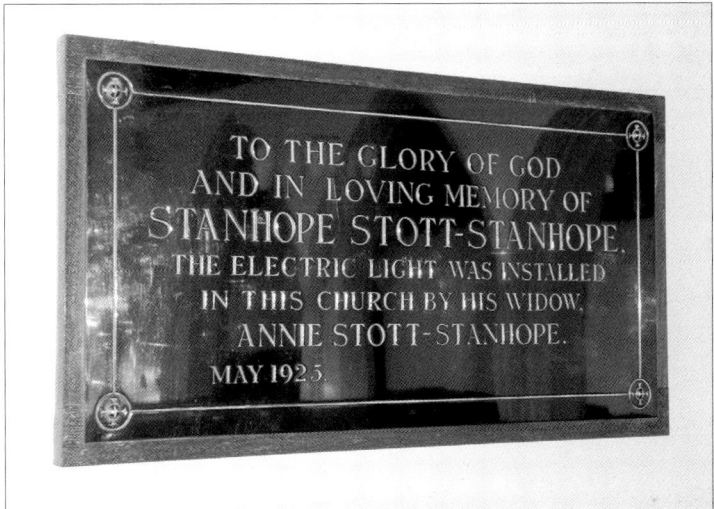

Brass memorial
plaque in Tutshill
Church.
R Clammer

APPENDIX TWO

TIDENHAM CLERGY

PERIOD	VICAR OF TIDENHAM
1339	Anselm of Leycestra
1339 - 1344	Nicholas Rocoff
1344 - 1345	John of Caumpeden
1345 - 1348	Nicholas Rocolf?
1348	William of Hereford
1362	Richard of Norton
1370	Nicholas Tullor
1384	John Yevan
1391 - 1392	Thomas Brugge
1392 -	John Stawell
1393 -	John Buttiller
1393 April-June	Peter Waryn
1393 June - July	John Wyles
	Richard Jehell (or Jekyll)
	John Podenhall
	John Collying
	Walter Trelewith
	Reginald Tyler
1420- 1445	John Marketsed
1445 -	Maurice John
- 1515	Thomas Kemeys
1515 - 1539	David ap Howell
1539 - 1554	William Lyving
1554 -	Thomas Fawkener
561 - 1570	John Jaques
1570 -	Edmund Arundell
1628 -	John Pitt

1668 - 1709	Richard Bedford
1709 -	Thomas Hodgson
1731 - 1768	Somerset Jones
1769 - 1802	William Seys
1802 - 1839	Thomas Thomas
1839 - 1842	William Pulling
1842 - 1845	James Henry Scudamore Burr
1845 - 1854	John Armstrong
1854 -	Octavius Goodrich
1854 - 1862	Allan Cowburn
1862 - 1884	Percy Burr
1884 - 1896	John Stafford Hilliard
1896 - 1900	Vincent Charles Reynell
1900 - 1909	Robert Charles Lynch Blossa
1909 - 1914	Clement Victor Stillingfleet
914 - 1931	Reginald Pemberton Steer
1931 - 1935	Sidney George Bush
1935 - 1957	George Richard Newman
1958 - 1975	Gwilym Howell Rowland Morgan
1976 - 1980	Joshua John Gerwyn James
1980 - 1991	Michael Terrance Gee
1991 - 1997	Brian Robert Green
1997 - 2011	Royston Grosvenor
2012 -	David Treharne

Reverend Armstrong (1845-54) .

APPENDIX THREE

GLOSSARY

Abbey	Church and associated buildings occupied by monks or nuns.
Abutment	The portion of a wall or pier that sustains one side of an arch.
Alien priory	A monastery or nunnery governed by a prior or prioress which was dependent upon a foreign mother house to which dues were sent.
Altar	Flat topped block or table for offerings to the deity. In catholic churches in stone, often in wood in protestant churches.
Anchorite	Often a hermit, or recluse. A person of who has withdrawn from secular society to live a prayer- orientated life.
Anglican	Adherent of the reformed Church of England or a descriptive of it.
Anglo-Catholic	Anglican holding that the Church of England is a branch of the Catholic Church and rejecting its Protestant element.
Anglo-Saxon	i) The architectural style of the period prior to the Norman conquest in 1066. ii) People who settled in Britain from the 5th century AD and were dominant until 1066 including the Angles, Jutes and Danes.
Arcade	A row of arches on columns.
Ashlar	A masonry wall of accurately squared stones with a smooth face, laid in regular courses with fine joints.
Assart	A piece of land cleared of trees and bushes and fitted for cultivation, a clearing. Assart land: forest land cleared of woods and brush. To assart land is to clear it of woods and bush.
Aumbry	Closed recess or cupboard in the wall of a church used for the safe-keeping of sacred vessels or alms.
Baluster	A short pillar with curved outline.
Ball flower	13th to 14th century ornament, carved regular intervals along a hollow moulding resembles a spherical, three lobed flower, opened to show enclosed ball or sphere.
Band	A plain or moulded flat strip or string course running horizontally across the surface of a building.
Baptistry	Part of the church used for baptism.
Bar tracery	In the ornamental intersecting work of a window, screen or panel, the curved members are carved into the same mouldings as the vertical posts or other uprights (mullions)dividing the window, creating a flexible pattern with a flowing line.
Barrel Vault	Simplest form of vault, consisting of a continuous run of semi-circular or pointed sections, unbroken in its length.
Battlement	A raised decorative wall with indentations in a church used to conceal the eaves of the roof.
Bay	Division of wall between columns or buttresses.

Belfry	A bell tower or chamber housing the bells.
Bell cote	Shelter for a bell which is smaller than a belfry and more often open to the weather e.g at St John's or St Luke's churches.
Bench end	The end of a bench or pew, often carved with great imagination and beauty during the late Gothic period with floral decoration.
Benedictine	Monastic order founded by St Benedict in 529AD, with an interest in education. Monks wear black and were at Chepstow (Striguil) Priory.
Boss	The central keystone of a vault where ribs often meet. Often highly decorated and carved.
Brace	In a timber roof, a strut serving to stiffen and strengthen the vertical and horizontal members.
Bronze Age	The period when bronze was used predominantly as a metal. It preceded the Iron Age and lasted from about 5000-2000 BC.
Byzantine	Architectural style developed in the eastern Roman Empire centred on Byzantium.
Capital	Decoration at the top of a pillar.
Catholic Church	The universal church or the whole body of Christians. i) before the separation into the Greek and Latin Churches. ii) The Latin church e.g Roman Catholic. iii) A church claiming continuity with the Catholic church.
Celtic Church	The early church under Celtic dominance in Brittany, Wales, Ireland and Scotland until the Synod of Whitby in 644AD destroyed its influence in favour of Rome. Local sites at Lancaut, Caerwent and Llandogo.
Chantry chapel	A chapel, often in a cathedral or church, where masses were regularly said or chanted. It sometimes contained the tomb of the donor.
Chapel-of-ease	A church or chapel built some distance away from the parent church
Choir	That portion of the church which is especially reserved for choristers- usually between the nave and the sanctuary.
Chancel	An area reserved for the clergy in the far eastern part of the church which includes the sanctuary.
Cistercian	A silent order of monks founded at Citeaux, south Dijon, in 1098 and noted for agriculture, industry and water engineering, as at Tintern Abbey.
Confessional	A closed stall in a Roman Catholic church in which the priest hears secret confession.
Corbel	A projection built into a wall as a bracket to support a beam or truss.
Credenza	a small side table for Eucharistic elements of the Holy Communion service.
Cruciform	Cross-shaped especially in a church ground plan.
Curvilinear	A flowing phase of Decorated architecture in the 14th century with "S" shaped, flame like tracery.
Cusp	Projections that divide the parts of tracery called foils.
Decorated	Type of English architecture of the 14th century.
Dentil	A small block used in rows, resembling a row of teeth in a classical or even Romanesque moulding.
Dissenter	A member of a sect that has separated itself from the Church of England, usually on the Protestant wing.
Dog toothed	Ornamental moulding much used around arches during the 13th century. A row of pyramidal projections each carved into four leaves.

Domesday	The statistical survey of England ordered by William 1 in 1086, initiated at Gloucester in St Peter's Abbey.
Drip mould	A stone moulding also called label, hoodmould or dripstone, projecting over and around the heads of door and window openings to throw off rainwater.
Early English	The first phase of Gothic architecture c 1190-1310. Characteristic features are lancet windows, plate tracery, stiff leaved carving and rib vaults.
Encaustic	Tiles used as floor and wall covering inlaid with decorative patterns in different coloured clays and then fired.
Evangelical	A term generally used to denote the wing of the church that returns to basics and the study of the scripture while emphasising praise through hymns with a more outgoing and non-traditional form of worship.
Font	A large receptacle in stone, bronze or lead, for baptismal water.
Frontal	Covering for the front of an altar.
Glebe	i) A piece of land belonging to a church and given over temporarily to a member of the clergy to provide additional income. ii) Arable land or soil especially when considered as a source of abundant natural produce.
Gothic	The pointed-arch style of architecture in the middle ages. A renaissance term of abuse for mediaeval art, "Gothick" is the 18th and 19th century Gothic revival associated with Romanticism.
Groin vault	The intersection of two tunnels or barrel vaults.
Iconoclasm	The breaking of images, especially religious sculpture. Also the general destruction prevalent during the Reformation in the 16th century and in the English and continental civil and religious wars of the 17th century.
Impost	The upper course of masonry of an abutment, a portion of a wall or pier that sustains one side of an arch.
Iron Age	The era which followed the Bronze age in about 10,000BC.
Keystone	A wedge-shaped block of an arch that locks it into place.
Lectern	Sloping reading or singing desk in a church.
Liturgy	Form of public worship. There is a set of formularies for this e.g the Book of Common Prayer.
Lych Gate	The roofed gateway of the churchyard where the coffin awaits the arrival of a member of clergy.
Mass	Roman Catholic and High Anglican celebration of the Eucharist. High Mass is sung, possibly with incense and music and Low Mass is generally said with the minimum of ceremony.
Monk	Member of a community of men living apart from the world, under the vows of poverty, chastity and obedience. Most orders follow the Rule of St Benedict.
Mullion	A vertical post or other upright dividing a window into smaller areas called lights.
Narthex	A lobby, entrance or porch typical of early Christian churches, often separated from the body of the church by a screen or rail.
Nave	The body of a church from the west door to the chancel. Usually visually and sometimes physically separated from the chancel by a screen and separated from side aisles by an arcade.
Non-conformist	One who does not conform to the doctrine or discipline of an established church.

Norman	The phase of Romanesque architecture in Britain following Anglo-Saxon in 1066 and continuing until about 1093 with a transitional phase reaching c1140.
Nucleated	A settlement clustered round a central point such as a cross roads, village green or church.
Oblate	Person or priest dedicated to a monastic or a religious life e.g the Oblate of St Mary Immaculate, the Order founding the church of the Sacred Heart at Sedbury.
Oculus	Circular, or wheel, often at the top of a window grouped in threes.
Ogee	An "s" shaped moulding showing in section a double continuous curve concave below and convex above. Characteristic of late Decorated architecture.
Oratory	Small chapel or place of worship.
Oxford Movement	A movement in the 19th century English high church against liberalism and for primitive, sacramental Catholicism promoted by Newman, Pusey and Kemble. Known as Tractarian, they and others including the Rev. Armstrong of Tidenham, published 90 tracts between 1833 and 1841.
Parapet	Wall carried up to conceal roofs and gutters. Often crenellated with gargoyles projecting.
Parvise	Enclosed area in front of a church or room over a church porch.
Perpendicular	Third stage of Gothic architecture, from the 15th to the 16th centuries. Often with vertical tracery in large windows.
Piscina	Perforated stone basin near an altar in the chancel or a chapel usually on the south wall.
Presbytery	Eastern part of the chancel, beyond the choir sanctuary.
Presbyterian	One governed by the elders, all of equal rank. Represented by the United Reformed Church since 1972.
Presented	A term to describe the process of appointment of a new vicar to a parish by a patron who had the power of presentation, sometimes on behalf of another person.
Prior	A superior officer of a religious house. In an Abbey, it is the post below the Abbot.
Priory	Monastery or nunnery governed by a Prior or Prioress e.g Striguel Priory in Chepstow.
Protestant	An individual or church which adheres to the reformed doctrine in opposition to the rule of the Roman Church.
Psalter	A book containing music for chanting the psalms.
Pulpit	A raised, enclosed platform usually with a desk from which the preacher in a church or chapel delivers a sermon.
Putlog	A short timber projecting from a wall on which scaffold floor boards rest. Hence "putlog hole" where the timbers were inserted.
Quarry	i) An unglazed floor tile. ii) A diamond shaped pane of glass as used in lattice windows.
Quoin	A dressed stone at the angle of a building.
Rector	A member of the clergy in charge of a parish who was appointed directly by a landowner, which could be a religious house such as an Abbey.
Reformation	A 16th century movement for the reform of doctrines and practises of the Roman Church, ending in the establishment of the Protestant church.

Renaissance	The revival of art and letters under the influence of classical models in the 14th, 15th and 16th centuries which led to the development of a style of architecture and art.
Reredos	An ornamental screen covering the wall at the back of an altar.
Rib	In architecture, a projecting band across a ceiling or vault which is usually structural but sometimes purely decorative.
Roman Catholic	A church or individual member of a church which is under the supreme authority of the Pope in Rome, stemming from St Peter.
Romanesque	A style of architecture established during the Anglo-Saxon and Norman period 1050-1200.
Sacristan	An officer charged with the care of a church and churchyard, often with duties as bell ringer and grave digger.
Sacristy	A place where the sacred vessels of a religious place are kept.
Sanctuary	An area to the far east of a church where the altar stands and where the sacred vessels are kept.
Sedilia	Seats in the chancel or sanctuary area for the use of the clergy.
Spandrel	The triangular space between two arches and the beam or course of masonry they carry.
Stiff leaf	A late 12th and early 13th century type of foliage sculpture, found chiefly on capitals at the top of pillars and bosses.
String course	A continuous projecting horizontal band set in the surface of a wall and usually moulded.
Tabernacle	An ornamental recess or receptacle to contain the Holy sacrament or relics.
Table tomb	A chest shaped stone coffin with a flat table top lid, resembling an altar but not used as one.
Terrier	A silver plate.
Thurible	A receptacle in which incense is burned and swung.
Tie beam	A horizontal transverse beam in a roof, connecting the feet of the rafters, usually at the height of the wall plate.
Tithe	A form of early taxes taken in goods.
Tracery	The ornamental intersecting work in the upper part of a window, screen or panel and sometimes used decoratively in blank arches and vaults.
Tractarian	An adherent of the 19th century high church "Oxford Movement" whose leaders wrote numerous tracts, espousing their theories.
Transitional	A term usually referring to the architectural period of transition from the Romanesque to the Gothic as seen at St James church, Lancaut.
Transept	The transverse or cross arms of a church, usually between the nave and the chancel.
Troper	A manuscript with sequences for singing the mass.
Vault	An arched roof or ceiling of stone or brick.
Vestry	i) Room or building attached to a church in which vestments (clerical attire) is kept. ii) The church office. iii) A meeting of parishioners on parochial business.
Vicar	A member of clergy appointed originally on behalf of a distant third party owner such as a religious house.
Voussoir	A wedge shaped block of stone in an arch.
Wheel window	A circular window, or oculus, with mullions radiating from its centre, like the spokes of a wheel.